PHILIPPIANS:

REJOICE IN THE LORD

Ray Frank Robbins

Phillippians 4:4

*"Rejoice in the Lord always;
and again I say rejoice."*

Convention Press • Nashville, Tennessee

Contents

This book is the text for a course in the subject area Bible Study of the Church Study Course.

Target group: This book is designed for adults and is part of the Church Study Course offerings. The 1963 statement of "The Baptist Faith and Message" is the doctrinal guideline for the writer and editor.

Dewey Decimal Classification Number: 227.6
Subject Heading: Bible. N.T. Philippians
Printed in the United States of America.

A WORD TO BEGIN ...

Philippians ... is a simple, spontaneous, informal, affectionate, and undogmatic letter with no formal instruction and nothing resembling an exposition of Christian doctrine. Its exhortation and ethical appeal are expressed in general terms. A friend simply poured out his heart to those he loved.

With this observation, Dr. Ray Frank Robbins sets the tone for his warm, penetrating study of Paul's letter to the Philippian Christians. Dr. Robbins is professor of New Testament and Greek at New Orleans Baptist Theological Seminary.

This textbook can be used in personal or group study. In both uses, the Personal Learning Activities at the end of each chapter will help the learner review the material covered. When study is done in a group, the companion Teaching Guide and the Study Guide will supply helpful resources to teacher and member. Guidance for using Personal Learning Activities in this textbook is in the section headed "The Church Study Course" at the back of the book.

Also at the back of the book is a Church Study Course Credit Request (Form 151). On completion of this book study, the pupil should mail in the completed form to the address indicated. Two copies of the credit award will be mailed to the applicant's church—one for the church's record, the other for the pupil's.

ELI LANDRUM, JR., editor

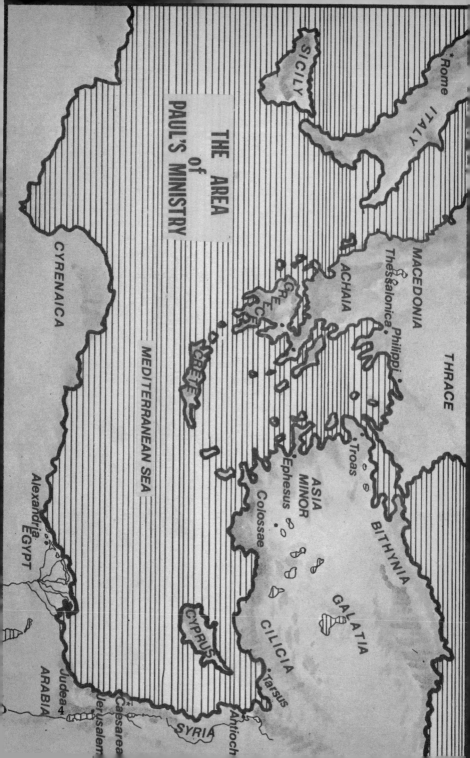

THE AREA of PAUL'S MINISTRY

Rome

ITALY

SICILY

MACEDONIA

THRACE

Thessalonica

Philippi

ACHAIA

GREECE

Troas

BITHYNIA

Ephesus

ASIA MINOR

Colossae

GALATIA

CRETE

MEDITERRANEAN SEA

CYRENAICA

CILICIA

Tarsus

CYPRUS

Antioch

Alexandria

EGYPT

Caesarea

Jerusalem

SYRIA

Judea

ARABIA

4

1

Saints in Christ in Philippi

Philippians 1:1-2

In the introduction of his letter, Paul did not feel compelled to declare his apostleship or to assert himself (vv. 1-2). He declared that he and Timothy were "servants of Christ Jesus." As a servant of Christ, Paul wrote to his dear friends in the Philippian church. The believers in this church were in the world but were not of the world. (See John 17:14-16.) Their lives were hidden in Christ. Three times in verses 1-2, Paul reminded his friends of Jesus Christ. The church was the living body of Christ and partook of his grace and peace.

A Love Letter

Philippians is a love letter written by a friend to his friends. Paul wrote this brief letter to his dear friends in Philippi. Between Paul and the Philippian Christians existed a bond of friendship that was closer than any which existed between him and any other church. None of Paul's other letters is as tender or abounds with such expressions of kindness and personal devotion.

With his Philippian friends, Paul shared his circumstances as a Roman prisoner. He expressed his inner peace and joy which he experienced in spite of his afflictions. The apostle told them of his uncertain future and expressed gratitude for their gifts. He reminded them that he had been unwilling to receive financial help from other churches; but, because of the Philippian Christians' affectionate and trusting friendship, he had accepted help from them several times.

Paul assured the Philippian Christians of the Roman Christians' sympathy and declared that he always remembered them in prayer with joy and thankfulness. With great tact, he urged his readers to be of one mind.

Paul wrote as one who was sure of his place in his readers' hearts, and he wanted them to know the place they held in his heart. He unburdened his heart by revealing his private convictions and inner struggles. He filled his writing with joy, peace, and thanksgiving. The word *rejoice* occurs eleven times in 104 verses, and the word *joy* occurs five times.

A Real Letter

Philippians shows no conventional or studied style. It is a simple, spontaneous, informal, affectionate, and undogmatic letter with no formal instruction and nothing resembling an exposition of Christian doctrine. Its exhortation and ethical appeal are expressed in general terms. A friend simply poured out his heart to those he loved.

The topics discussed swing backward and forward between what concerned the saints in Philippi and what concerned Paul. Paul was interested in their concerns, and he knew they were interested in his. These shifts from Paul's situation to the Philippian Christians' condition are roughly as follows: (1) thanksgiving and prayer for the Philippian Christians, 1:3-11; (2) personal information about Paul, 1:12-26; (3) exhortation and counsel to the Philippian Christians, 1:27 to 2:18; (4) personal information

about Paul, 2:19 to 3:1; (5) warnings and exhortations to the
Philippian Christians, 3:2 to 4:9; (6) Paul's gratitude for their
affectionate gift, 4:10-20.

The Writer and His Readers (1:1)

Paul, the Writer

Paul (his Roman name), or Saul (his Hebrew name), was a Jew
who was born about the year A.D. 1. He was the most dynamic
and influential of Christ's early followers. Paul was a native
citizen of Tarsus, capital of the Roman province of Cilicia (Acts
22:3). His parents were Pharisees (Acts 23:6) of the tribe of
Benjamin (Phil. 3:5). According to Acts, he probably spoke
Aramaic, Hebrew, and Greek (Acts 21:37, 40; 22:2). Paul's family
is unknown except the mention of one sister (Acts 23:16). From
his father, he inherited both Tarsian and Roman citizenship
(Acts 22:28). He learned the tentmaking trade because the Jews
believed in bringing up their children in some honest calling.

When Paul was about twenty years old, he attended the rab-
binical school of the Pharisees and studied under the famous
rabbi Gamaliel of Jerusalem. In this school, he obtained a thorough knowledge of the Jewish religion. Having a hot and fiery
temper, he became a champion of the law of Moses and the
traditions of the elders. He considered this fanaticism for the
Law and the traditions to be a zeal for God. This zeal made him
impatient of all opposition to the tenets he had learned. Therefore, he persecuted the Christians who were considered to be the
enemies of the Jewish community.

Paul aided those who stoned Stephen (Acts 7:58; 8:1). After
Stephen's death, Paul became the principal agent in persecuting
the Christians. He searched for the saints in Jerusalem, beating
some in synagogues, inflicting other punishments, confining
some in prison, and having others put to death. He applied to the
Sanhedrin and received a commission to extend his persecution
to Damascus. Yet, about A.D. 35 when his persecuting efforts
were at their height, Paul was converted to Christ on the Damascus road (Acts 9:1-19).

After his experience on the Damascus road, Paul spent some
time reconstructing his theology (Gal. 1:17). Then for about ten
years, he was engaged in Christian missionary effort in Asia,
Macedonia, and Greece. He established churches, wrote letters,
and collected money to help the poor saints in Jerusalem. When

he delivered a sum of money to Jerusalem, he was arrested by the Romans and charged by the Jews. After a two-year imprisonment in Caesarea, he made his "appeal unto Caesar" (Acts 25:11) and was taken to Rome. When he wrote the letter to the Philippian Christians, he was still in prison in Rome. (Some New Testament scholars suggest Caesarea or Ephesus as the place of writing.)

In Paul's day, the normal way to start a letter was with the writer's name, the name of the recipient, and words of greeting. Paul followed this practice by starting with his name in 1:1. He united Timothy's name with his in the salutation; however, the letter was distinctly Paul's writing.

Timothy, by his presence and support, helped Paul in his imprisonment. He seems to have held first place in Paul's affection. Timothy's grandmother and mother both were Christians (2 Tim. 1:5). On Paul's second missionary journey, Timothy joined Paul and Silas (Acts 16:1-3). From that time, he became Paul's close friend and helper. He was well known to the Philippian Christians; he had been with them often and soon was to visit them again (Phil. 2:19-23).

Paul designated himself and Timothy as "servants of Christ Jesus" (v. 1). He did not call himself an apostle because he did not need to assert his official designation to his readers. The designation "servants" or slaves was familiar to the members of the church; many of them were, or had been, slaves. The term denotes dependence, obedience, and acknowledged ownership. It indicates intense devotion and willing obedience, which is perfect freedom.

Saints in Christ Jesus

Paul addressed the members of the church as "saints" (v. 1). The term means holy or set apart for God's use. The Greek word sometimes is translated saints and other times is translated holy. Perhaps the translation "saints" cannot be improved. However, we must guard against the idea that sainthood implied moral attainment. A rendering such as consecrated ones may bring out more clearly the relation to God.

We must keep in mind that setting apart an individual as one of God's company springs not from the individual but from God. Primarily, to be a saint is not to be good but to be set apart by God as his; but holy character ought to be a mark of God's person.

In the Old Testament, the word *saint* was used to designate Israel. Israel was a covenant people, a holy nation, consecrated as God's peculiar possession. In the New Testament, the term appears over sixty times as the customary description of the Christian believer. Paul frequently used the term "saint" in the opening words of his epistles (Rom. 1:7; 1 Cor. 1:2; 2 Cor. 1:1). He used the word as a general name for his converts, like the word *Christian*. Thus, Paul was not writing to a select group in the church but to the whole church.

The Philippian church members were "saints" because they were "in Christ Jesus" (v. 1). The phrase "in Christ," or similar expressions, occurs over a hundred times in Paul's writings. "In Christ" occurs repeatedly in Philippians. The phrase is the most comprehensive description of the Christian that appears in Paul's epistles. It touches every aspect of what God has done for the Christian, of what the believer now enjoys, and of the prospect opening out before the Christian in time and eternity. It seems to be original with Paul. With this phrase, he described the closest conceivable union between the saint and Christ. More than any other conceptuality, this phrase describes the fundamental experience of the Christian religion. Paul seemed to have included two ideas in his phrase "in Christ." These two ideas are expressed in his classic statements, "Therefore, if any one is in Christ, he is a new creation; the old has passed away, behold, the new has come" (2 Cor. 5:17), and "Christ in you, the hope of glory" (Col. 1:27).

First, Paul set forth a soul union between Christ and the believer. This is a subjective experience. God in Christ shares his life with the person, and a living union takes place. By uniting his life with a human being, God creatively brings new powers into play and so alters the person's life. Emil Brunner summed it up: "God's nature . . . as it was revealed in Jesus Christ is to be seen in just this, that he communicates himself, that he lets man share in his life."[1]

Though the phrase "in Christ" probably was Pauline, the concept most likely came from Jesus. The parable of the vine and the branches, with its reiterated emphasis "abide in me, and I in you," gives special stress to this truth (John 15:1-11). The writer of 1 John described Christians as abiding in God and God as abiding in Christians.

Union with Christ is accomplished by God's grace through faith. Faith is the principle which unites Christ and the believer. It is the channel through which God enters a person's inner being. Faith expresses the self's abandonment to God. In fact, faith was the early Christians' favorite word to express their union with Christ. Paul insisted that by faith, he continued to partake of the new life in Christ. The word *faith* (*pistis*) was used to express a variety of concepts; however, *pistis* is related to *peithō*, from a stem meaning to bind. The primary thrust seems to be to unite.

Alfred H. Ackley gave his testimony of the indwelling Christ in his life:

> He lives, He lives, Christ Jesus lives today!
> He walks with me and talks with me along life's narrow way.
> He lives, He lives, salvation to impart!
> You ask me how I know He lives: He lives within my heart.[2]

Second, Paul used the idea of the new life in Christ to refer to the believer's life actualized in the church. The idea of newness was eschatological. The prophets looked forward to a day when God would accomplish a new thing (Isa. 43:19; Jer. 31:22). God promised a new covenant (Jer. 31:31-34; Ezek. 34:25; 37:26) and a new song (Ps. 96:11). He assured his people that he would implant a new heart and a new spirit within them (Ezek. 11:19; 18:31; 36:26) and that he would call them by a new name (Isa. 62:2). God also promised to create a new heaven and a new earth (Isa. 65:17; 66:22).

Christ brought new life to individuals by sharing God's life with them, and he brought new life to the world by starting a new community, the church. In Christ, the new age has broken into the old age. Deliverance is available from the present evil age (Gal. 1:4). Therefore, to be in Christ practically is equivalent to being a member of God's people, the company of the redeemed. Ministers who guide the members of the church do so "in Christ" (1 Cor. 4:15). The church is one body "in Christ" (Rom. 12:5). All believers are one "in Christ Jesus" (Gal. 3:28). Gentiles and Jews are fellow-heirs, members of the same body, and partakers of the promise "in Christ Jesus" (Eph. 3:6). Therefore, believers are "in Christ" not only as individuals but as a community.

Saints in Philippi
Philippi was located about ten miles from Neapolis, the seaport, on the River Gangites. The city was named after Philip II of

Macedon, Alexander the Great's father. Philip founded it on the site of an ancient city named Krenides or The Little Fountains for the purpose of working gold and silver mines. The famous battle which determined the destiny of Rome was fought near Philippi in 42 B.C. In this battle Brutus and Cassius, defenders of the Roman republic, were defeated by Anthony and Octavian. Anthony settled some of his disbanded veterans in the area. Twelve years later, after the defeat and death of Anthony, Octavian (now Augustus Caesar) enlarged the colony of Philippi. He gave it the title of Colonia Julia Augusta Philippensis. As a Roman colony, it reproduced Rome's institutions and imitated the city's dignity.

Philippi's population was composed of three main elements: the Romans, the dominant caste; the native Macedonians, numerically the largest number; and a considerable number of Orientals. Few Jews seem to have lived in Philippi.

Philippi was situated on the Egnatian Way, the magnificent highway which stretched from Dyrrachium on the Adriatic Sea to the Hellespont (Dardanelles). Along this great Roman thoroughfare ran currents of life which brought to Philippi representatives of all races and religions.

Paul and Philippi

Paul's first visit to Philippi is recorded in Acts 16. When he started his second missionary journey, he meant to confirm the churches that had been established (Acts 15:36,41). However, he was under divine guidance to continue his travel. Barriers were placed in his way; yet, Paul was guided onward (Acts 16:6-8). At Troas, Paul with Silas, Timothy, and Luke responded to the Macedonian call for help (vv. 9-10).

Some interpreters think that Luke was the "man of Macedonia" (Acts 16:9) who alerted Paul to the opportunities in Macedonia and urged him to minister there. At any rate, an open door to a new field presented itself, and Paul entered it.

The Jewish community in Philippi was so small that it did not have a synagogue, only a place of prayer on the bank of the river (Acts 16:13). Here, on a sabbath, Paul and his helpers began their ministry in Philippi. Lydia, a woman from Thyatira in Asia, was the first convert that Luke mentioned (Acts 16:14). She was not a Jewess, probably not even a proselyte, but likely a God-fearer who had become attached to Judaism. Her entire household was baptized with her. Lydia's house became the meeting place for the infant church.

The masters of a slave girl made their livelihood by exploiting her powers of divination. They were enraged when Paul, in the name of Jesus Christ, caused her to lose her gift. They dragged Paul and Silas before the magistrates and charged them with sedition, at the same time playing on the anti-Semitic prejudices of their fellow citizens (Acts 16:20-21). The result was that Paul and Silas were whipped, thrown into prison, and expelled the next day.

In Philippi, Paul had accomplished a remarkable mission. He had made friends for life. Through the remainder of his life, the Philippian Christians remained his "joy and crown" (Phil. 4:1). He visited them as often as he could. At a critical time when he was anxious about the results of a painful letter to the Corinthians, he left Ephesus and went into Macedonia (Acts 20:1; 2 Cor. 7:5). This doubtless meant a visit to Philippi. Three months later (Acts 20:3), he was on the way to Jerusalem from Corinth and spent the "days of Unleavened Bread" in Philippi (Acts 20:3-6).

After his probable release from imprisonment in Rome, Paul visited Philippi at least once and possibly twice (1 Tim. 1:3; 2 Tim. 4:13). The Philippian Christians had a large place in Paul's heart.

The prominence of the church in Philippi ceased with Paul's life. It was not mentioned again until more than fifty years after Paul's death. After a few references in early church history, it sank into obscurity. No church has existed in Philippi for ages, nor does the city exist any longer. "Born into the world with the brightest promise," wrote J. B. Lightfoot, "the Church at Philippi has lived without a history and perished without a memorial."[3]

Bishops and Deacons

Paul did not address officers of any other church to whom he wrote. Possibly bishops and deacons were mentioned in Philippians (1:1) in recognition of their position and standing in the church. Probably, they had taken the initiative in gathering the money that the church sent to Paul when he was in the Roman prison and on previous occasions. Paul wanted to express his appreciation to them.

In the New Testament, the titles bishop, pastor, elder, or presbyter refer to the same office (Acts 20:17; 1 Tim. 3:1-7; Titus 1:5-7; 1 Peter 5:1-2). The word "bishop" means overseer. Apparently these ministers exercised spiritual guidance in the churches. The presence of more than one overseer shows the desirability of having many persons in a congregation charged with its spiritual oversight.

The deacons also were ministers in the church. The word "deacon" (*diakonos*) means servant. The institution of this function sometimes is related to the account in Acts 6:1-6. However, Luke did not use the word *deacon* when referring to the seven men. He wrote that immediately after their selection, two of them—Stephen and Philip—started preaching. Paul used the word *diakonos* to refer to civil magistrates (Rom. 13:4), to describe his helpers in his mission work (Eph. 6:21), and to describe his ministry (1 Cor. 3:5). He even used it to describe Jesus' ministry (Rom. 15:8). In the early church, a deacon was a minister of Christ.

The Salutation (1:2)

The form of Paul's salutation (1:2) may have been suggested by the combination of ordinary Greek and Hebrew greetings. In Greek, the word "grace" was used for greeting. "Peace" was the customary Hebrew greeting. Paul combined the everyday greetings and transformed them into the distinctive message of God's forgiving love toward all people in Christ.

The salutation is an exclamation, a declaration, a wish, and a prayer. Paul did not use a verb in this statement; he never used verbs in his salutations. However, a verb probably should be supplied.

The word translated "grace" had a long history before it became one of the New Testament words. It first meant charm, gracefulness, pleasantness, attractiveness, thankfulness. It never lost this sense of loveliness. A secondary meaning was goodwill, loving-kindness, favor. Later, it was used to express the results of a person's goodwill. Sometimes, it was used to refer to the thanksgiving a person expressed. The New Testament writers built on these pre-Christian foundations.

In the New Testament, the word *grace* is given a Christian content. It generally is used to express God's characteristic attitude toward every person. It describes God's spontaneous, unmotivated action. This action is not caused by anything a person is or does. Grace is not given because of virtues nor withheld because of vices. It often is used to delineate the redemptive activity of divine love revealed in Christ. God always is the source from which grace comes to people; Jesus is the means by which grace reaches people.

The word grace occurs more often in Paul's writings than in the rest of the New Testament. It occurs about a hundred times in his thirteen epistles. In the salutation of Philippians, Paul expressed his prayer that his friends might know more of God's grace, forgiveness, acceptance, help, and comfort.

To his prayer for grace, Paul added a prayer for peace. He would have his friends know the peace which Christ had given to him. This prayer for their peace was not a prayer for the cessation of struggle against evil. That struggle would continue. The prayer was for peace in relationship to God in Christ, and in that relationship peace with each other.

Peace in the New Testament must not be understood as simply the absence of conflict or the mere cessation of antagonism between people. It is included in the salutations to those who were being persecuted. God's grace naturally produces peace. Enmity against God has ceased; reconciliation has followed. In the New Testament, peace never means a retreat from life but rather a spirit which possesses the soul. The person may be in the midst of pain, conflict, or difficulty and still have peace (Phil. 4:7).

The divine order is grace and peace, and the order never can be reversed. The divine order, logical and chronological, is also the experiential. People without God in their lives have no peace. First, persons must receive grace from God; then peace follows. When people receive grace, peace comes to their hearts. Grace is the fountain, and peace is the stream which issues from this fountain.

The source from which Christians receive grace and peace is "God our Father and the Lord Jesus Christ" (v. 2). The Father is the origin and Christ is the medium through which these blessings come. All the blessings which God bestows on Christians come as gifts of the exalted Christ. These blessings do not come from the world, or from circumstances, or from the inner self, but only from God.

Notice how closely Paul identified the Father with the Lord Jesus Christ. He introduced them in the same connection and with reference to the giving of the same blessings. If the mention of "God our Father" in this salutation implies a prayer to him, the mention of the "Lord Jesus Christ" implies the same. Paul did not think that he was being untrue to the unity of God when he spoke of Jesus as divine.

Jesus was the human name of the Savior (Matt. 1:21); "Christ"—the Anointed One—was his official title. Lord was the title which often was used of God in the Old Testament. Paul repeatedly used this title for Jesus in Philippians; he referred to Jesus Christ numerous times by name in the letter. This salutation points the readers to the heart of the letter in which Paul expressed his love for his friends and revealed his experience in the knowledge of Christ.

Lessons for Life from the Scriptures

Christ did not redeem Christians from sin, the curse of the Law, and the fear of death so that we would be uncontrolled, but so that we might belong to him. Christians must see themselves as faithful slaves of Christ. True freedom—the freedom to become all that Christ can make us—comes when we become Christ's bondslaves. The paradox—slavery that is the only real freedom—is creative because the Master in the relationship acts in grace.

Saintship is a reality for every Christian because of the regenerating grace of God in Christ. Every Christian is set apart to God, separated to his service. We struggle with wrong in ourselves, and we work to respond to God's direction and people's needs. We are saints, not because we are superlatively good, but because we are called to salvation and to ministry in Christ's spirit.

The Christian life guarantees no exemption from conflict. Christ gives the believer peace—all that makes for the person's highest good. In conflict, facing threat, struggling with difficulty, Christians are supplied grace and the promise of the Presence. The assurance of sufficient grace allows us to face life squarely, with confidence.

1. Emil Brunner, *The Letter to the Romans* (Philadelphia: Westminster Press, 1959), p. 29.

2. "He Lives" W/M A. H. Ackley, Copyright 1933 by Homer A. Rodeheaver. (c) Renewed 1961, The Rodeheaver Co. All Rights Reserved. International Copyright Secured. Used by Permission.

3. J. B. Lightfoot, *Saint Paul's Epistle to the Philippians* (Grand Rapids: Zondervan Pub. House, 1953), p. 65.

Personal Learning Activities

1. In Philippians 1:1, Paul called Timothy and himself _____ of Christ Jesus. (Choose the proper response from the following list.)
   - (1) Missionaries
   - (2) Disciples
   - (3) Slaves
   - (4) Partners
2. Ray Robbins calls Philippians a _____ . (Select the correct answer from the following list.)
   - (1) Sermon
   - (2) Tract
   - (3) Love letter
   - (4) Theological treatise
3. Match the following two lists, linking those words and phrases which give correct facts about Paul.

   _____ (1) Saul
   _____ (2) Tarsus
   _____ (3) Benjamin
   _____ (4) Aramaic
   _____ (5) Roman citizenship
   _____ (6) Tentmaking
   _____ (7) Gamaliel
   _____ (8) Stephen

   (a) Tribe to which Paul's parents belonged
   (b) One of three languages Paul probably spoke
   (c) Paul's trade
   (d) Paul's famous teacher
   (e) Stoned while Paul watched and approved
   (f) Paul's native city
   (g) Paul's Hebrew name
   (h) Inherited from his father

4. Paul called the Philippian Christians saints because they were (select one):
   _____ (1) Morally good
   _____ (2) Pious and prayerful
   _____ (3) In Christ
   _____ (4) Superior Christians
5. Philippi was a _____ . (Choose the proper answer from the following list.)
   - (1) Roman colony
   - (2) Seaport
   - (3) Commercial center
   - (4) Largely Jewish city

Answers
1. (3); 2. (3); 3. (1)g, (2)f, (3)a, (4)b, (5)h, (6)c, (7)d, (8)e; 4. (3); 5. (1).

2

Partnership in Christ

Philippians 1:3-11

The salutation in Paul's letter to the Philippian church is followed by a great burst of joyful love in 1:3-11. In these nine verses, a beautiful combination of thanksgiving and prayer occurs. Paul put them together because with him, these were not separate.

Paul expressed his great joy over the Philippian saints' largeheartedness. He expressed his gratitude for the evidence which they had given of their love for God. He also gave thanks for their faithfulness to the gospel from the time when it first was preached to them. The Philippian Christians were enshrined in Paul's memory; he had them all in his heart (v. 7). They never were absent from his prayers.

Paul prayed that the Philippian Christians' spiritual life would increase until they were developed richly in love, knowledge, and spiritual sensitiveness. He also prayed that they would be prepared, at "the day of Christ" (v. 10), to glorify God by their lives' rich fruitage of righteousness.

Past Remembrance (1:3-5)

Remembering in Gratitude

All of Paul's letters except Galatians, 1 Timothy, and Titus begin with thanksgiving. In Paul's day, that was a conventional feature of letter writing. In Philippians, the thanksgiving is especially earnest and warm. The earnestness of thanksgiving is seen in the reiteration which runs through the paragraph. The Philippian

Christians had been one with Paul in missionary work, and he saw that as God's gracious act.

Paul said, "I thank my God in all my remembrance of you" (v. 3). With the phrase "my God," Paul evidenced the most personal and close faith alliance with God. This was his testimony to his friends in Philippi. This confession would revive in his memory such experiences as his conversion on the Damascus road, his call to preach the gospel, and his service for Christ. It also would bring to mind again all the outstanding occasions when God had revealed himself to Paul as his God. God, to Paul, was "the God to whom I belong and whom I worship" (Acts 27:23).

Paul knew the Philippian saints well, and he cared for them with a sincere, self-sacrificing affection. He worked for them while he could, and while he was in prison he did not forget them. Though he was some distance from them, they were not out of his thoughts. His thoughts were not taken up with his hardships and dangers. His thanksgiving was based on his entire remembrance of them (literally, all the remembrance). The Greek text emphasizes Paul's habit of remembering them rather than single times of remembrance.

Prompted to Prayer
In verse 4, Paul stated that his interest in the Philippian Christians moved him to pray. His habit was to pray for them. And when he prayed for them, his remembering them called forth his thanksgiving, which gave a tone of joy to his prayers. He indicated that he never prayed for them without giving thanks with joy. The stress in the sentence is on thanksgiving for all the saints in Philippi rather than prayer for all.

The word for "prayer" in verse 4 primarily implies an expression of need. In the New Testament, it always is addressed to God, but it is not necessarily intercession. It implies not merely lifting up one's heart to God, but entreating God for a blessing. Paul never prayed without mentioning the Philippian saints, and his prayers were filled with joy because of what God had done and would do in and through them.

Paul's prayers for his readers overflowed from a joyful heart. Nothing in their fellowship hindered his emotions of gratitude and praise. He never thought of them or prayed for them without thanking God for them. He reminded several churches that he prayed for them (Rom. 1:8-9; 1 Cor. 1:4; Eph. 1:15-16), but he

18

indicated that the church in Philippi was the one for whom he joyfully prayed.

Joy is one of the two dominant notes in the letter. The word *joy* occurs in Philippians as a verb or a noun sixteen times. In verse 4, "joy" is emphatic by its position in the sentence. Though Paul was a prisoner, exposed to the depression caused by isolation, joy mingled with all his prayers. He was a happy prisoner in Rome as he had been in Philippi.

The experience of joy is one of the characteristic elements in the Christian life. Christian joy is no mere gaiety that knows no gloom; it is the result of faith's triumph over adverse circumstances. Often these circumstances, instead of hindering joy, enhance it.

A constant repetition of the word *all* occurs in Philippians. By this repetition, Paul seemed to stress that he made no difference between his readers. His heart was open to all. His prayers, his thanksgiving, his hopes, and his obligation extended to all of them. This recurrence also is to be connected with the strong and repeated exhortations to unity which Philippians contains (1:27; 2:1-4; 4:2-3). Unity and joy are the two dominant notes in the letter.

Sharing in the Gospel

The preceding clause, "making my prayer with joy," is a parenthesis; thus, verse 5 should be taken in connection with verse 3. In verse 5, Paul expressed to his Philippian friends the immediate reason for his thanksgiving and joy. It was their "partnership in the gospel from the first day until now." These Christians had shown themselves to be true missionaries by the sympathy and help they had given to Paul as he preached the gospel. They had manifested this partnership from the first day they had heard the gospel. (See Acts 16:15.)

The word "partnership" (Phil. 1:5) is a translation of the Greek word *koinōnia*. To find an exact equivalent in English for the Greek word is difficult. It is translated as partnership, fellowship, communion, fellow-working, and sharing together. *Koinōnia* comes from the Greek word *koinos* which is related to the English word *common*. The Greek word *koinōnia* means sharing or participating with someone in an experience.

Paul used *koinōnia* thirteen times in his writings. He used the word in verse 5 to denote participation in the widest sense. The Philippian Christians' "partnership" included: (1) their accept-

19

ing the gospel in faith; (2) their identifying with the aims of the gospel; (3) their active witness in Philippi; (4) their cooperation in preaching and teaching the gospel; (5) their participation in suffering; (6) their expressions of sympathy for Paul in his work; and (7) their sharing in other Christians' needs. (See Rom. 15:26.)

The saints in Philippi especially had helped in sharing the gospel by demonstrating Christ's power in their lives. They had put a powerful argument into Paul's preaching. In witnessing to others, he could point to what Christ had done and was doing in and for them. They also had helped by their prayers on Paul's behalf.

Paul was conscious that the Philippian Christians were close to him in their goals and objectives. In everything that pertained to the gospel, they shared a common interest with him which they showed in every suitable way. This consciousness of their "partnership in the gospel" caused gratitude to well up in Paul's heart.

The Philippian Christians had shown their "partnership in the gospel" repeatedly by sending Paul funds to meet his needs (Phil. 4:14-18). The church, though poor, had "overflowed in a wealth of liberality" (2 Cor. 8:1-3). These funds relieved Paul from the necessity of working and put him in a better position for furthering the gospel. Paul was unwilling to accept even the bare necessities from other churches, but he never had had any fear that the Philippian Christians would suspect him of preaching the gospel for money.

The Philippian Christians' contributions were signal instances of their "partnership in the gospel" and seem to have been foremost in Paul's mind when he wrote. In this particular way, they had cooperated from the first when he had departed from Philippi. They even had sent funds to him when he was in Thessalonica (Phil. 4:15-16). They continued to send money when he was in Corinth (2 Cor. 11:7-10). The latest expression of their sharing was the contribution Epaphroditus brought to Paul in prison in Rome (Phil. 4:10).

Paul's gratitude for the gifts was not because of any favor the Philippian Christians had shown to him as a man but as Christ's minister laboring for the gospel. Whether he fared well or not, lived or died a martyr, mattered little to him. But because he was entrusted with the gospel, he felt the continuation of his life to be for the common good (Phil. 1:24-25). Therefore, he felt that the

Philippian believers' gifts were not for his sake but for the sake of the gospel.

Future Expectation (1:6)

In verse 6, Paul expressed his confidence about the future. His remembering the Philippian Christians was with thanksgiving and joy; his anticipation for them was with thanksgiving and assurance. From the evidence of their Christian calling's reality, Paul drew the conclusion that Christ was at work in them and that he would complete his work. Paul had three grounds for this confidence: (1) God's faithfulness which made Paul's confidence certain; (2) Paul's love for them which made his confidence becoming; and (3) the Philippian Christians' faithful lives which made it likely.

God's Ongoing Work
Paul's readers had given ample proof of their faithfulness; yet, he put his confidence in God, not in them. Without God's help the Philippian Christians' future would have been uncertain, but Paul was sure that God would help. Paul knew that God is not one who begins but fails to finish. God loves finished works. (See Rev. 3:2.) Incompleteness in any divine work is only a promise of subsequent perfection. God's plans are not formed so poorly that they fail.

The Greek word translated "I am sure" denotes confidence. In every case in the New Testament, the word indicates a feeling of personal certainty. Paul trusted God's grace and power. He was sure that God would complete what he had begun in the Philippian believers. However, this confidence did not prevent Paul's praying for them or exhorting them to diligent effort. God was the one who "began a good work" in Paul's readers. A divine enabling is absolutely necessary for a person to begin the new qualitative life.

The "good work" refers to the "partnership in the gospel" mentioned in verse 5. It includes both the Philippian Christians' inward spirituality and their sharing with Paul in furthering the gospel. The "good work" was a comprehensive work of grace affecting both their inner selves and outward manifestations. It was the fruit of divine action.

God's "good work" in the Philippian Christians was not complete. He would continue it until it was fulfilled. It would continue in the stability of God's purposes, the power of the Holy Spirit's influence, and the nature of the covenant under which the Philippians were placed.

In verses 5-6, Paul linked human perseverance ("your partnership") with divine preservation ("he who began a good work in you will bring it to completion"). That God brings his transforming work to completion in the lives of those in whom he lives is true. That Christians are not passive spectators of the change is equally true. Preservation is accomplished through faith. Divine preservation and human perseverance are for the purpose of service.

The teaching of divine preservation and human perseverance is prevalent in the Bible (Pss. 89:33; 138:8; John 3:16; 4:14; 6:37, 39; 10:28). Christians, left to themselves, could not stand or persevere; but helped by God, they can continue "steadfast, immovable, always abounding in the work of the Lord" (1 Cor. 15:58). The ground for their perseverance is not in their watchfulness or strength, but in God's indwelling Holy Spirit. The Greek words translated "began" and "completion" are technical terms which were used to indicate the beginning and ending of sacrifices. Paul and his readers were familiar with such language, and the words would suggest that they were to present themselves "as a living sacrifice, holy and acceptable to God" (Rom. 12:1).

Paul mentioned two points of time in verse 6: "began" and "day of Jesus Christ." He said that between these two points, God would complete his work. This work of God refers primarily to a new moral nature "which is being renewed in knowledge after the image of its creator" (Col. 3:10). The renewal of the new person designates gradual renewal of the character; this is actualized progressively in the church.

The Day of Jesus Christ
The expression "day of Jesus Christ" suggests a day of trial in which every Christian's work will be tested. Paul mentioned this "day" about twenty times in his writings. As to the details of the "day of Jesus Christ" (v. 6), Paul had no fixed eschatological system. (Eschatology is the study of last things. "Eschatological" means relating to last things, having to do with the consummation.) He did not know if it were near or far off. He did not say that he would be alive when it comes. He merely stated what the ones who are living when the day comes will do (1 Cor.

15:51; 1 Thess. 4:17). For all practical purposes, to the individual Christian that "day" is the day of death.

In Jewish thought, time was divided into the present, evil age and the age to come, or the Messianic age. The age to come or Messianic age was to be inaugurated by the Messiah (Christ). Jesus was the Messiah, and the age of the Messiah came with him. The incarnation marked the entrance of the kingdom of God or the age to come into the present, evil age (Mark 1:15). The age to come overlapped the present, evil world. This overlap is of uncertain duration and will continue until Christ's second coming.

This present, evil age will come to an end with the day of the Lord, which for Paul was also the day of the Lord Jesus Christ. The second coming will end the present age. Paul wrote of the future era as the "age . . . to come" only once (Eph. 1:21), but he frequently wrote of the eschatological kingdom of God. For Paul, the eschatological kingdom of God meant the complete destruction of every power that was or is hostile to God's will, the last of which was death (1 Cor. 15:23-26). Christ "must reign" until this redemptive goal is reached (1 Cor. 15:25). In this basic eschatological structure of the two ages divided by the day of the Lord, Paul agreed with contemporary Jewish thought.

Present Devotion (1:7-8)

In 1:7-8, Paul turned from his future expectations for the Philippian Christians to a tender expression of his love for them. He justified his joyful confidence, his thanksgiving, and his prayer for his readers on the ground of his love for them as participants with him in God's grace. He was persuaded that his feelings arose from no human impulse. God's grace had given the Philippian Christians this place in his heart, and they had evidenced their participation with him in that grace.

Partakers of Grace
In verse 7, Paul stated that for him to cherish a warm love and deep trust towards his readers was only fair. He did not claim credit for this feeling. He wrote: "It is right [morally obligatory] for me to feel thus about you all." His failure or refusal to thank God for them would have been inexcusable. His refusal to pray for them, to rejoice because of them, to express confidence in them—while convinced of their loyalty to God and to him—

would have been improper.

The Greek word rendered "to feel" is used frequently in Philippians and also in Romans. It always refers to a habitual conviction or a state of mind. Paul's feelings for the Philippian believers were especially right for him because of the intimate relationship he had with them.

Between Paul and the Philippian Christians existed the most thorough sympathy and togetherness. They sorrowed over his imprisonment and shared with him in all his work. In the Greek, his expression of their togetherness can be rendered: I am holding you in my heart, you being my fellow-partakers of grace [as evidenced] both in my imprisonment and in the defense and confirmation of the gospel (v. 7).

The Greek words translated "defense" and "confirmation" (v. 7) are technical legal terms. Paul may have used them to refer to his first trial before Nero when he was abandoned by those who should have stood by him. If this is the case, the thought is that in making his defense he was vindicating the gospel which he preached and was guaranteeing that it was truly the gospel of God.

Paul may have used "defense" and "confirmation" in a more general sense. He may have intended to describe his twofold method of carrying on the work of the gospel. In that case, the "defense" would be his effort to answer objections and to remove obstacles to the gospel. The "confirmation" would be his effort to establish and confirm the believers' faith. The "defense" would refer to the negative side of his preaching and the "confirmation" to the positive side. Paul regarded his being permitted to preach the gospel and to suffer for the gospel as a grace. The Philippian Christians had shared in this grace of God by participating in Paul's ministry and trials.

No matter which experience Paul had in mind, his Philippian friends had shared in it with him. When he defended the gospel, he was emboldened by the thought of their unwavering confidence in him. Also, when he engaged in the confirmation of the gospel he was indebted to them because he could point to the power of the gospel in them.

The natural meaning of "partakers with me of grace" (v. 7) is that the Philippian Christians' sympathy and assistance had united them with Paul. In this sense, they were bound with him and felt the power of God with him. The phrase is a grateful recognition that they were one with him in spirit, sustaining him

by their prayers and sympathy and being sustained by his cheerful steadfastness. In Greek, the word "grace" has the article and should be translated, the grace. This indicates that the grace is God's grace, a divine privilege. The grace applies equally to the "imprisonment" and to the "defense and confirmation of the gospel."

The Philippian Christians had shared in grace because they had not been shamed or intimidated by their founder's imprisonment. Rather, they had identified with his cause. Through their participation in all that he suffered and did, they made themselves known to him as fellow recipients of grace. If they had not participated with him in receiving grace, they would not have participated in all that he suffered and did. He knew them to be sharers with him in the same divine grace which enabled him to labor for Christ. They had ministered to Paul in prison and had sustained him in his work, and he interpreted their action as a mark of divine favor.

The word translated "imprisonment" (v. 7) literally means bonds. This is the first allusion in Philippians to Paul's imprisonment.

Paul's Feeling for the Philippian Christians

In verse 8, Paul struggled to express his deep love for his friends in Philippi. Before he expressed his prayer for them in verses 9-11 that their love might increase, he described his love for them. He appealed to the fact that God, who judges people's hearts, knew how tenderly he loved them and how his love grew into a yearning for them. "For" refers to the previous statement—that he had them in his heart. The expression "God is my witness" (v. 8) is a solemn oath. Love longs for its object. Paul could call God to witness that he longed eagerly for the Philippian Christians. Karl Barth wrote: "God can stand witness for Paul's longing because it is his grace that forms directly the bond of the union which is the true reason for the longing."[1]

A reality, a uniqueness, and a peculiarity existed in Paul's love for all the Philippian Christians which made his love like Christ's love. Note again how Paul insisted repeatedly that what he said applied to all his readers. No exception was made. He loved every one of them.

The Greek verb translated "yearn" (v. 8) means to long for, to desire earnestly, to feel homesick tenderness. This verb was used to denote the Christian's yearning for heavenly rest and glory (2 Cor. 5:2), the Holy Spirit's yearning for the believer's spirit (Jas. 4:5), and the "newborn babes" longing for the milk of divine truth (1 Pet. 2:2).

Paul gave expression, not so much to the intensity of his love and yearning, but to their distinctive character by adding the phrase "the affection of Christ Jesus" (v. 8). In a deep mystical sense, Christ lived in Paul (Gal. 2:20) and, therefore, loved through him. Thus, the love spoken of in verse 8 is more than human love. It is not merely a love resembling Christ's, but actually Christ's love. Paul knew the deep yearning of love which he felt for his readers to be emotions, faint but true, from the heart of Christ dwelling in him. The Philippian Christians inspired Paul's Christlikeness. All that he had of Christ's life, spirit, ideas, purposes, and love were excited to a yearning for them when he thought of them. J. B. Lightfoot wrote: "The believer has no yearnings apart from his Lord; his pulse beats with the pulse of Christ; his heart throbs with the heart of Christ."[2]

The Greek word translated "affection" is *splagchnois*. The *splagchnois* were the heart, liver, and lungs of a human body. The Greeks believed these organs to be the seat of emotions and affection. Paul used this word to indicate Christian affection. This belief was similar to our belief about the heart. Paul used a physical term as a symbol of emotions. He felt the yearning of Christ's compassion stirring in him on the Philippian Christians' behalf, and he used the strongest figure at his command to express it. He used a powerful metaphor to describe a perfect union.

A genuine Christian is under the inspiration and control of the great moral passion of Christ. To the extent that a Christian is one with Christ, Christ's love goes out through that person to all people—all the people whom Christ loves, and all the people for whom Christ died.

Prayer for Spiritual Progress (1:9-11)

Verses 9-11 contain the substance of the prayer to which Paul alluded in verses 3-4. No doubt, the kindness which the Philippian Christians had shown to Paul prepared the way for him to speak of their love. Before he voiced his prayer for them that their love might increase, he described his love for them (v. 8), thereby setting an example of what love means to a Christian. However, the love discussed was not to be confined to their love of Paul or their love of each other. The reference of love here is much wider.

Life's Highest Principle
The reference in verses 9-11 is to a principle which operates universally. No object of the believers' love is mentioned. The stress lies in the fact that their character was to be marked by love which would reach out to any person or object—God, people, or

things. The Greek word used in verse 9 is *agapē*. It is not found in classical Greek. It seems to have been coined by those who translated the Old Testament into Greek. The ordinary Greek terms for love seem to have been too weak to express God's love. *Agapē* in a Christian's heart is the answer evoked by divine love which should be shown in love of the brethren. It is the divine demand flowing from the divine gift of salvation which constitutes the gospel. *Agapē* is not a vague feeling; it is to be patterned on Christ's love. Jesus said that *agapē* was a badge of Christian profession to the whole world (John 13:35).

In the New Testament, *agapē* is not a natural virtue which Christians can develop within themselves if they try hard enough. It is an eschatological reality, a quality of life, which even now "has been poured into our hearts through the Holy Spirit" (Rom. 5:5).

Agapē is a love of other people, not because they are lovable, but because they need love. *Agapē* is concern for others' best interests with no thought of benefit to the one loving and despite lack of response on the part of those loved. Frank Stagg described *agapē* as "the disposition to relate to others for their good, regardless of cost or consequence to oneself. It is the opposite to self-centeredness."[3]

Paul already had given the Philippian Christians credit for love in its manifestations. In verse 9, he assumed that their love existed. He even assumed that their love abounded. Still, he wished higher things for them in love. He prayed that their love for Christ, which had been shown in their deep, generous, and practical sympathy for him, might not continue only but might abound more and more. Paul was aware that love must grow, or it will lose its freshness.

The Philippian Christians' growth depended on the great principle of love, and Paul prayed for an increase of love in strength and power to produce results. The Greek word translated "abound" means to overflow, to superabound, and thus to go beyond measure. (See Phil. 1:26; 4:12; 1 Thess. 4:1.)

Paul did not pray for a mere increase of his readers' love, for this already was one of their distinguishing characteristics. He prayed for a development of their love in the direction of sound judgment and right moral perceptions. Their love needed to become more intelligent and discriminating. Paul probably was concerned over signs of growing conflict and disunity within the Philippian church. This concern caused him to stress the

29

necessity that love abound more and more "with knowledge and all discernment" (v. 9).

The word "knowledge" means a basic clarity of thinking. The word's structure suggests developed, full knowledge. According to Ralph Herring, "It [epignōsei] suggests knowledge heaped up as in a pile, one fact upon another, and the possessor on top of it all. A man in such a position is supported by all the facts in the case, and that is what Paul is after."[4] In the New Testament, this word for knowledge is used only of spiritual perception.

The word "discernment" describes the mind and heart's ability to separate the good from the bad, the important from the unimportant, and to choose the former. The word implies a sensitive conscience, a clear moral insight, and a delicacy of ethical tact. With increased love come clearer spiritual sight and hearing, a sense of the beauty of holiness, and a finer perception of Christian propriety. "Discernment" properly applies to the senses and seems to mean the insight which recognizes a truth as the eye recognizes an object.

Paul was eager that his readers' love be exercised with proper discrimination. Christians who possess love but lack "discernment" may have eagerness and enthusiasm. Their motives may be good and their intentions worthy; yet, they may be doing more harm than good. If love is the fruit of God's Spirit, it will lead to knowledge of God and to the discernment of what is pleasing to God. Paul insisted that the Philippian Christians were not to be creatures of circumstances or to be ruled by impulse or desire. Their love was not to be confused with unregulated, selfish passion. It was not to be blended with false reasoning.

Paul desired that abounding love with knowledge and discernment might be part of his readers' character. In verses 10-11, he described the kind of Christians he wanted them to be. He was not claiming that the Philippian Christians had some secret knowledge which their unsaved neighbors could not have. He indicated that the better things could be discerned only by the finer spiritual sense which came by an increase of love. He prayed that his readers' love would grow greater each day and that it would be intelligent and discriminating. He wanted them to develop a symmetry of Christian character. He knew that the Christian graces do not manifest imbalances or distortions, but that they grow harmoniously. He also knew that spiritual perception and symmetry of character could be developed only through active love.

Choosing the Best
In verse 10, Paul prayed that the Philippian Christians might have a finer spiritual perception so that they would prefer good to evil, the essential to the trivial. He asked that they might be pure and blameless in the day of Christ. He prayed that they would continue to learn to devote themselves to that which was highest and worthiest.

The Greek word translated "approve" was the word used to describe the testing of metals or coins to determine if they were genuine. Luke used the word in the sense of understanding the significance of (Luke 12:56) and putting to the test in practice (Luke 14:19). Paul employed the term in the sense of recognizing the quality of (1 Cor. 16:3) and approving of (Rom. 12:2). The word always had the idea of approval that followed testing.

The introductory phrase "approve what is excellent" also may be translated, distinguish the things that differ. The difference between the two statements is not great, for the ability to distinguish between good and evil would be for the purpose of rejecting evil and accepting good. However, the context better suits the translation "approve what is excellent" (v. 10). In this process of approving what was excellent, the Philippian Christians not only were to distinguish good from evil, but also the best from the good. To make these distinctions, they needed mature spiritual perception.

The Greek word translated "excellent" has the idea of distinctive and relative excellence, conspicuous among what is either defective or evil. It sometimes was used to describe that which was qualitatively superior (Matt. 6:26; 10:31). In Philippians 1:10, the idea seems to be the better course or the superior conduct. Paul wanted his friends in Philippi to be characterized by their recognition and practice of higher levels of life in all situations. Thus, in their difficult task of deciding which of two apparent but opposing duties to choose, they would be guided by the principle of love.

The desired result in the Philippian Christians' spiritual perception was lofty. They were to be "pure and blameless for the day of Christ, filled with the fruits of righteousness which come through Jesus Christ, to the glory and praise of God" (vv. 10-11). The word translated "pure" appears only in verse 10 and in

2 Peter 3:1 in the New Testament. It may come from two Greek words which mean sunshine and judge. If this is the derivation, the word describes that which is able to stand the test of sunshine. If this is the meaning, Paul meant that Christian character can stand any light that is turned on it without any flaw appearing. The word "pure" may come from another Greek word which means to whirl around as in a sieve. If this is the derivation, it means that the Christian character is cleansed of all evil.

Whichever metaphor Paul had in mind, he meant that the Philippian Christians were to live genuine, incorruptible lives. He was describing the kind of life that leads Christians to sacrifice all that they have, even life itself, rather than turn from the true and right.

A day is coming, "the day of Christ" (v. 10), when people will be revealed for what they are. This is Paul's second reference in this paragraph to that "day" (v. 6) and shows the influence the day had on all his thinking and labors.

The Fruits of Righteousness
Paul was not satisfied with purity and blamelessness for his friends; he desired a fullness of the Christian graces for them (v. 11). He concluded his prayer by beseeching God that the ultimate purpose for all that he had asked for them might end in "the glory and praise of God." The "fruits of righteousness" are the fruits which righteousness produces. The word "fruits" is singular in the Greek, denoting a collective idea. The result of love's increase and operation in a Christian's life is the preservation of that life from the power of evil. In the person's inner self and external conduct, he or she is blameless. The Christian also brings forth the fruit which is natural to righteousness. This righteousness is not the activity of self-improvement, self-discipline, or obedience to a rule or a law. It is the relational activity which is produced by the indwelling Christ. Only this kind of righteousness, which springs from Christ's abiding presence, can show "the glory and praise of God" (v. 11).

Paul prayed that the hearts and lives of the Philippian Christians would yield a rich spiritual harvest consisting of the fruit of the Spirit. That harvest would consist of "love, joy, peace, patience, kindness, goodness, faithfulness, gentleness, self-control" (Gal. 5:22-23).

The Greek word *doxan* translated "glory" meant the opinion which people form of things or persons, and it also was used for the reputation which these acquired in consequence. In the New Testament, *doxa* acquired a special meaning derived from the Old Testament word *kabod,* which meant weight or heaviness. God's weight or character is exercised in his sovereign power. This is manifested in the creation and government of the world. God is glorified when he reveals his character and attracts people to him, and when his character then is reproduced in them.

Lessons for Life from the Scriptures

A sense of our being partners in the gospel would move Christians to a greater appreciation of each other. God has called believers to the grandest work of all: his redemptive purpose. We enter into partnership with others who are involved in ministry. In the partnership of the gospel, we give and receive; we share with each other what we can offer. If we can see one another as partners in service, we can move together toward the high mark of spiritual maturity and can work together effectively.

As Christians, we are unfinished personalities. God has begun a good work in us; he has called us to redemption and to ministry for him. But we live in a creative tension; we are in process; we are being moved by God toward the pattern we see in Christ. We are engaged in growth, progress that is sometimes slow and painful. But we live in hope: What God has begun, he will complete.

Christians' lives—and their life together—must be marked by God's kind of love. When we experience God's love extended to us in Christ—his accepting the unacceptable—we begin to approach others in love. Disciplined, determined care that does not give up easily becomes characteristic of the way we live. To some degree, and sometimes to a large degree, we can make God's love believable to our world by a goodwill and compassion that are not discouraged easily.

---

1. Karl Barth, *The Epistle to the Philippians* (Richmond: John Knox Press, 1962), pp. 19-20.
2. J. B. Lightfoot, *Saint Paul's Epistle to the Philippians* (Grand Rapids: Zondervan Publishing House, 1953), p. 85.
3. Frank Stagg, "Philippians," *The Broadman Bible Commentary,* Vol. 11 (Nashville: Broadman Press, 1971), p. 188.
4. Ralph A. Herring, *Studies in Philippians* (Nashville: Broadman Press, 1952), p. 46.

Personal Learning Activities

1. Paul's sincere thanksgiving at the beginning of Philippians was unusual since he customarily did not include such expressions in his letters. True _____ False _____
2. The church in Philippi was the only one for whom Paul indicated that he prayed with _____ . (Choose the correct answer from the following list.)
   (1) Tears   (3) Sorrow
   (2) Joy   (4) Anger
3. Paul indicated that the good work begun in the Philippian Christians would be completed. The basis of his confidence was (select one):
   _____ (1) His ability
   _____ (2) Their faithfulness
   _____ (3) God's grace and power
   _____ (4) Timothy's assistance
4. According to Dr. Robbins, for all practical purposes the day of the Lord for the Christian is _____ .
   (Select the proper response from the following list.)
   (1) The second coming   (3) The day of death
   (2) The final judgment   (4) Every day
5. In the New Testament, _agapē_ is (choose one):
   _____ (1) A natural virtue one can develop
   _____ (2) An emotion or good feeling
   _____ (3) God's kind of love
   _____ (4) Physical attraction

3

Victory in Christ's Service

Philippians 1:12-26

Paul's writings are full of autobiography. His theology often was the generalization of his experience, for he felt and verified in his life whatever he said. However, in Philippians, his personal experiences have a distinctive character. In this letter, he unveiled his inner self in response to what he knew to be the Philippian Christians' eager desire for news of his welfare.

The passage 1:12-26 is an interpretation of the events since Paul left Philippi. It includes a description of his condition and a revelation of his thoughts during his imprisonment. He was waiting to be tried by Nero. However, he gave no indication of defeat. His body was bound; his spirit was free.

The Philippian Christians were not to think that Paul's arrest and imprisonment had stopped the gospel's progress. Instead of his bonds hindering the gospel's progress, they had extended it. In fact, his imprisonment had destroyed some barriers. Some preachers in Rome were unfriendly, but Paul was confident because they were preaching the gospel. His sufferings had inspired some preachers to more boldness.

The passage 1:12-26 contains much more than extracts from the diary of a great apostle; it offers an example of true Christian service. The passage also gives a statement of principle for the guidance of all Christians.

Triumph in the Past (1:12)

Verse 12 is a notable illustration of the truth set forth in Psalm 76.

In this psalm, the writer stated that in God's overruling providence he makes even people's wrath to praise God (Ps. 76:10). The psalmist declared that the wicked plot against God, seek to injure his servants, and obstruct the progress of his truth. However, when they expect to reap the harvest of their evil ways, they encounter defeat. God takes all that they meant for the suppression of truth and right to promote the triumph and progress of truth and right. God overrules their evil when he has some good object in view. Thus, in verse 12, Paul declared that God had used the obstacles set up by evil persons to hinder and stop the progress of the gospel, to promote the gospel. Paul was bound, but the gospel could not be bound (2 Tim. 2:9; Isa. 55:11).

The opening statement of verse 12, "I want you to know," alerted the readers to the fact that Paul was about to express something which they would not find self-evident. Introductory statements of this kind called attention to something of great importance (Rom. 1:13; 1 Cor. 10:1).

The word "brethren" was a term of endearment and indicated that Paul regarded his readers, as well as himself, as children of the same Father. Paul used this word eight times in Philippians. The early Christians adopted this term to express their love for each other in Christ. In subsequent times, it was adopted as the language of brotherhood in the church. The growing conception of the church as a brotherhood in Christ was the outcome of the Christian view of believers as a household (Eph. 2:19).

The phrase, "what has happened to me" (Phil. 1:12), refers to a long chain of events in Paul's life. Paul meant all that had occurred between his departure from Philippi with the collection to help the poorer Jerusalem saints and the writing of the Philippian letter (Acts 20:6 to 28:31). When he left Philippi, he had been forewarned by the Holy Spirit that "imprisonment and afflictions" awaited him in Jerusalem (Acts 20:22-23).

Trouble had come quickly after Paul had arrived in Jerusalem. Though he did what James and the elders advised him to do to reassure the Jews of his reverence for the Law (Acts 21:23-26), he was accused falsely by his own people (Acts 21:28). The "Jews from Asia" recognized him in the Temple and made a murderous assault on him (Acts 21:27-31). He was rescued, with difficulty, from a religious mob by Claudius Lysias and the Roman guard. Paul escaped a flogging only by pleading his Roman citizenship (Acts 22:22-26). He was tried before the Sanhedrin without verdict (Acts 23:1-10). Furthermore, he was made the subject of unjust and unprovoked insult and shame (Acts. 23:2), malicious misrepresentation (Acts 24:5; 25:6-7), and a deadly plot (Acts 23:12; 25:1-3).

Under cover of darkness, Paul had been sent from Jerusalem to Caesarea for safety (Acts 23:23-33). In Caesarea, he was tried by Felix the governor without a verdict (Acts 24:22-25). He was imprisoned for two years because of Felix's craving for popularity (Acts 24:27) and money (Acts 24:26), or because of a facade of legalism (Acts 26:32). Paul received no better treatment after Festus succeeded Felix as governor. The new governor failed to bring the case to trial; Paul exercised his right as a Roman citizen and appealed to Caesar (Acts 25:11). A short time later, Paul delivered a defense before Herod Agrippa II, in the presence of Festus (Acts 25:23 to 26:32).

Paul's hardships and sufferings had not ended. He was taken to Rome as a prisoner. On the way to Rome, he encountered a storm at sea (Acts 27). During this ordeal, his life was in peril both because of the storm (Acts 27:20) and because of the soldiers' plan to kill the prisoners (Acts 27:42). His ship was wrecked, and he spent the winter on the island of Malta (Acts 27:44b to 28:10). In the spring, he reached Rome (Acts 28:14).

In Rome, Paul's difficulties still had not ended. He had arrived in a company of prisoners, bound by a chain; he was destined to remain in military custody for at least two years. During these two years, he waited for the uncertain decision of Nero, the Roman emperor. Nevertheless, he looked back over all that had happened to him since he left his friends in Philippi and wrote: "What has happened to me has really served to advance the gospel" (Phil. 1:12).

Paul's enemies probably were saying that what had happened to him was proof of God's displeasure with him and his interpretation of the gospel. In the light of such claims, the Philippian Christians·had addressed questions to Paul concerning his experiences and the effect of those experiences on the cause of Christ. These questions would account for the suddenness of the transition in verse 12. Paul assured his readers that Christ's cause had benefited by the events which culminated in his imprisonment in Rome.

The Greek word translated "to advance" was a military term used to denote the progress of an army through a forest or over a mountain. Paul's experience had had the same effect on the gospel as the work of an engineer had on an army's progress.

Instead of his imprisonment and afflictions being a hindrance, they had been an advantage. Of course, this advance of the gospel was due to God's overruling providence.

Victory in the Present (1:13-18)

Paul's problems did not end when he was imprisoned in Rome (Acts 28:16), and God's overriding providence did not cease to make people's wrath praise God.

Paul had formed the habit of turning opposition into opportunity. He did not dwell on his difficulties or hardships in prison. He described his situation, not as one of despondency, but as one of hope and even of success.

Positive Results of Imprisonment

Paul's imprisonment and the cause of it had become known "throughout the whole praetorian guard" (v. 13). (The Greek literally is, in the whole *praitōriōi*.) The Greek word *praitōrion* properly denotes the general's tent in a military camp. Paul probably used it in verse 13 to refer to the ten thousand picked soldiers who were stationed in Rome to guard the emperor. Some of these soldiers, no doubt, guarded Paul by turns. In this way, many of them had contact with him. They took note of his patience, courage, and loyalty to convictions. They listened as he talked with friends who came to visit him and as he prayed. So the news about Paul spread from soldier to soldier, to the families of the soldiers, and thus to the inhabitants of Rome in general. The phrase "to all the rest" (v. 13) is an indefinite expression; it seems to mean everyone else who was concerned with the disposition of the case against Paul. Paul did not mean that the soldiers and others were becoming Christians. He meant only that he had succeeded in making them realize that his sole offense was preaching the gospel.

Another result of Paul's imprisonment was to encourage the "brethren"—not all of them, but most of them (v. 14). Most of the "brethren," seeing the spirit in which Paul endured his imprisonment for Christ's sake, became more courageous. They were affected by his fortitude in the face of danger. Instead of his bonds hindering the gospel's progress, they had stimulated the labors of other Roman Christians. He had given them an example of heroism in the face of danger.

Some interpreters have suggested that the "brethren" had

been unduly timid before this time. Rather, their courage had risen to new heights when they might have been intimidated. Paul's example made them confident. They knew that he was suffering for the gospel and that he was supported in his sufferings by the grace of Christ. When they observed his courageous endurance for Christ's sake, they were encouraged. The words "in the Lord" (v. 14) describe the cause; the words "because of my imprisonment" (v. 14) describe the occasion of the brethren's confidence.

Christ Proclaimed Through Contrasting Motives

In verses 13-14, Paul indicated two favorable results of his imprisonment experiences. In verses 15-18, he stated a third reason for his joy and optimism: Christ was being preached.

In verse 15, Paul stated that preachers in Rome were engaged actively in preaching the gospel, but not all of them were actuated by the same motive. Some of them were actuated by "envy and rivalry" (v. 15). Seemingly, some preachers in Rome were jealous of Paul's influence and supposed that his imprisonment furnished a good opportunity to diminish that influence and to strengthen their case.

The preachers cannot be identified with our available information. Their difficulty seems to have been entirely in their motives, not in their doctrine. Not the content of their message, but the spirit in which they approached their preaching was faulty.

Probably, highly regarded and well-established preachers were active in Rome before Paul arrived. After he reached Rome, some of these preachers felt that his renown had overshadowed them. They resolved to show that they could be as bold and as successful in evangelistic efforts as he was.

That Paul's imprisonment experiences should tend to spread the gospel is paradoxical. A still greater paradox is that the gospel of peace and love should be preached out of "envy and rivalry." Other preachers preached out of "good will"; that is, in full sympathy with the spirit that motivated Paul. The "good will" (v. 15) was extended not merely to Paul but also to his work.

Some Greek texts reverse verses 16 and 17. The preachers with "good will" were described further as preaching Christ "out of love" (v. 16). They had pure motives, and they felt sincere affection for Paul. They did not begrudge him the authority which he exercised by divine appointment, the gifts he had received from God, or the honor bestowed on him by many Christians. These preachers of goodwill regarded Paul as being imprisoned unjustly. While he was in jail, they willingly aided him in the great cause to which he had devoted his life. They were convinced that Paul had a destined place in God's plan; they recognized him even in prison as a champion of the gospel. These preachers redoubled their efforts to preach so that the gospel would lose nothing because of Paul's imprisonment.

The preachers described in verse 17 are the ones described in verse 15 as preaching from "envy and rivalry." The Greek word translated "partisanship" literally means to work for hire. It developed into the usage of hired canvassing or other party work. Finally, it was used in the sense of partisanship. Paul did not accuse the preachers to whom reference is made in verse 17 of hypocrisy, but of narrow-minded partisanship and personal hostility.

Perhaps the phrase "thinking to afflict me in my imprisonment" (v. 17) describes the envious preachers' efforts to influence Paul's jailors so that they would prevent him from preaching (Acts 28:30). If they could prevent inquirers or converts from seeing Paul, they could diminish his influence.

The preachers of "partisanship" did not succeed in disturbing Paul (v. 18). He rejoiced in their efforts, even though their efforts were prompted by party spirit and hostility to him. He did not rejoice in their wrong motives, but he rejoiced that Christ was being preached. With whatever motives they were animated, the preachers proclaimed Christ. Paul brushed aside all that was antagonistic to him personally to rejoice that Christ was being proclaimed. What really mattered to him was not what the preachers were doing to him, but what they were doing for the gospel.

Confidence in the Future (1:19-26)

Paul's Ultimate Deliverance
Not only was Paul rejoicing in prison, but he was confident that he also would rejoice in the future (v. 19). His enemies could not destroy his joy.

Paul was confident that his imprisonment with its perplexities and annoyances and his adversaries' personal antagonisms would turn out to his "deliverance" (v. 19). The word "deliverance" literally is salvation. However, in verse 20, Paul expressed what he meant by this word: "Christ will be honored in my body, whether by life or by death."

Paul sometimes used the verb *saved* to refer to the beginning of the new life in Christ. (See Rom. 8:24.) This usage described the event when a sinner was saved from sin's penalty. He also used the word meaning to save to indicate the Christian's present and progressive life. (See 1 Cor. 15:2.) This usage described the Christian's deliverance from sin's power. Paul also used the verb, to save, in the future tense to refer to the Christian's eternal, blessed hope. (See Rom. 5:9.) This usage described the Christian's deliverance from sin's presence. In verse 9, the word "deliverance" combines the second and third usages. With the word *salvation*, Paul described his truest welfare, his highest good, Christ's being magnified more than ever in him.

Paul mentioned two factors which would be instrumental in turning his unfavorable circumstances into his welfare. The first of these was the Philippian Christians' prayers. He was confident that his Philippian friends would pray effectually for him.

The second factor was the "help of the Spirit of Jesus Christ" (v. 19). In the Greek text, the Philippian Christians' prayers and the Spirit's help are classed together so that they are practically one.

Paul's Expectation and Hope

In verse 19b, Paul ascribed his confidence to the power of the Spirit of Jesus working in him. In verse 20, Paul wrote that he had an "eager expectation" and a well-founded "hope" that the Spirit never would put him to shame. The Spirit never would allow Paul to seek an easy or selfish way out of his imprisonment. On the contrary, the Spirit would equip him "with full courage." Paul was not afraid of life or death. Either way, he wanted to magnify Christ in his body. If he were condemned to death, he would go to God with unwavering faith and with a song in his heart. If he were declared innocent and released, he would continue to preach. Either way, Christ would be honored.

The Greek word translated "eager expectation," which in the New Testament occurs only in 1:20 and in Romans 8:19, means literally watching with outstretched head. This word describes attention concentrated on one object. Paul said that his eyes, taken off everything else, were strained toward his life's supreme aim, which was to honor Christ.

Paul's hope was not that he would show himself a hero under the ordeal of the trial, but that whatever came Christ would be honored. If that could be achieved best by his being set free, he gladly would accept release from prison. If it could be achieved best by execution, he would accept a martyr's death. He was content to leave the issue in God's hands. He was willing to live if his ministry was needed for the spread of the gospel. He was willing to die if his death best would serve Christ's cause. The only shame for Paul would be his failure to stand firm in his loyalty to Christ. He was confident that God would not allow him to be intimidated at his trial before Nero.

Paul asked nothing for himself. He expressed no wish for personal safety and honor. His one concern was that he never falter in his witness for Christ.

To Live, or to Die

In verse 20, Paul had expressed his supreme resolve that Christ be honored in his body, whether it was by life or by death. In verse 21, his writing became sketchy and broken as he balanced

"for me to Live is Christ, and to die is gain."

42

living and dying in his mind. He was aware that death was a possibility for him as a result of his trial. Therefore, he weighed the glory of living against the greater glory of dying, not knowing which to choose because each was wonderful. He was certain that he would gain either way the trial went. If he were found not guilty and released, Christ would continue as the aim and object of his life. Life was worth living only insofar as Christ's life was realized in his life. For Paul, living was so full of Christ that Christ summed up his life. He had no conception of living apart from Christ. Life was wonderful simply because it

was Christ-filled. However, dying also offered its advantage, its gain. Dying would be gain because Paul's union with Christ would be realized fully.

In the Greek, the broken construction in verse 22 reveals the great apostle's deep emotion as he considered the options of life and death. The exact meaning of the verse is difficult to determine; however, its general meaning seems to be clear. Paul was weighing the two possibilities of life and death, and he expressed doubt as to which he would choose if the choice were his. He did not know what was best, so he preferred to leave it with God.

In verse 23, Paul indicated his love for his Philippian friends by declaring that he was in tension between his "desire . . . to depart and be with Christ" which was for the "better," and his willingness to remain on earth for their benefit (v. 24). He declared that if only his desire were to be considered, his choice would be "to depart and be with Christ." To Paul, death was not a friend but an enemy. (See 1 Cor. 15:26.) However, he was not thinking primarily of dying but of life with Christ after death. Paul was confident that death would be an increase and progression in all that he enjoyed here in fellowship with Christ. Everything that was of real value to him was to be his after his death. Nothing was to be discarded, and whatever was kept would be increased. He was confident that as soon as he died, he would be "at home with the Lord" (2 Cor. 5:8). The New Testament gives no basis for the ideas of a long sleep of a soul between death and resurrection or of the conscious existence of a disembodied spirit.

The Greek word translated "depart" (v. 23) was used in different ways. It was used to describe breaking up an encampment. This metaphor would emphasize the fact that death was an experience of moving on (2 Cor. 5:1-8). It also was used to describe loosing a ship from its mooring. This metaphor was an appropriate symbol of a person's transitory life on earth. In addition, the word was used for solving problems. This usage would emphasize the fact that death brings solutions to problems that could not be solved before. But "depart" also was a political term. It was used to describe freeing a prisoner. God's people will experience greater freedom beyond death. Finally, "depart" was a word used by farmers. It meant to unyoke oxen.

Paul's Conviction of More Work to Do
For Paul, death would be taking down his tent, weighing anchor, solving life's problems, freeing him from bondage, and laying aside his burdens. For him, this would have been "far better" (v. 23). He saw clearly that to "depart" was for his advantage. But, at the same time, he saw that for him to live and continue his ministry was "more necessary" for the Philippian Christians (v. 24).

Though the Philippian church was a wonderful Christian community, it had its problems and was confronted with real dangers (3:1-3,19; 4:2). Accordingly, for the present, Paul was ready to forego his desire in order to help, if that was God's will. The Philippian Christians' needs weighed heavier with him than his desire. Of the alternatives—his desire for himself and the needs of his Philippian friends—Paul left no doubt concerning which he would choose.

Paul affirmed that his life was valuable to the Philippian Christians. He had no false pride when he wrote: "But to remain in the flesh is more necessary on your account" (v. 24). He knew

they loved him and depended on him for counsel, encouragement, guidance, and sympathy.

Paul was uncertain as to what he would choose, but he was
confident of what his future would be (v. 25). He was convinced
that he would survive his present imprisonment. The decisive-
ness of the phrase "remain and continue" shows that he anticipated a successful termination of his trial.

Paul had confidence that he would "remain" to help his
readers make progress and experience joy in their faith. He did
not want them to remain in their present state of development;
he wanted them to continue to grow in grace and knowledge. His
remaining also would contribute to their enjoyment ("joy") of
their faith.

Verse 26 further expands the thought expressed in the phrase
"more necessary on your account" (v. 24) and brings out more
clearly the purpose of Paul's remaining in the flesh. Paul expressed his joyful anticipation of visiting his Philippian friends
again. His reunion with them would bring them joy and would
be one more evidence of God's power in Christ over which they
could rejoice together.

Paul's statement of his confident hope forms the climax of his
message concerning his personal experiences while he was a
prisoner in Rome. If he were acquitted and released so that he
could visit the Philippian Christians again, they would have in
him grounds to boast in Christ Jesus. They would be able to see
in Paul's release Christ's working out his purpose.

The statement, "I know that I shall remain and continue with
you all" (v. 25), is an unqualified assertion. In the book of Acts,
Luke closed his account with Paul still in prison in Rome.
According to tradition, after two years in prison Paul was ar-
raigned before Nero and was acquitted. But since his continued
presence in Rome would have provoked his Jewish enemies to
fresh hostility, he was ordered to leave the city. Either before he
went to Spain or after a ministry in Spain, he fulfilled his promise to visit Philippi.

Paul's journey to the East included an evangelistic effort on
the island of Crete, where Titus was left in charge of the work
(Titus 1:5). After leaving Crete, Paul journeyed to Miletus where
he left Trophimus who was sick (2 Tim. 4:20). From Miletus, he
sent Timothy to Ephesus to be in charge of the work there (1 Tim.
1:3). Traveling north from Miletus, Paul stopped in Troas where
he was entertained by Carpus. He left his mantle and books with

Carpus (2 Tim. 4:13). Finally, he arrived in Macedonia and visited with his friends in Philippi (1 Tim. 1:3). He wrote 1 Timothy and Titus from Philippi. After his visit in Philippi, he went to Thessalonica where he was joined by Demas (2 Tim. 4:10). He continued his journey to Corinth. He went to Nicopolis, where he intended to spend the winter (Titus 3:12). In Nicopolis, he was arrested again and carried to Rome and imprisoned (2 Tim. 1:17). While in prison in Rome the second time, he wrote 2 Timothy. Most of his friends were gone (2 Tim. 4:9-11). At his second trial before Nero, he was condemned. He was executed, and his body was buried outside the walls of Rome, However, Paul had gained his desire "to depart and be with Christ" (Phil. 1:23).

Lessons for Life from the Scriptures

Whatever Christians' circumstances, they have opportunity for service. However believers may be hampered by conditions, they still may bear witness for Christ. Christians often are in circumstances over which they have no control, but they never need be under them. Christians need never give way to despondency but always can try to do good where they are, knowing that God can bring good out of evil.

The gospel is not preached always by well-trained, mature, properly motivated, effective preachers. Yet, to have the gospel preached in less than an ideal manner is better than not to have it preached at all. If Christians disagree with a preacher's theology or method, they can pray that God will use the preacher's ministry for Christ's glory.

Christians can have hope for their futures. Their hope is given by God and is based on his faithfulness. Things may not turn out as they had planned or wished, but believers will be supplied sufficient grace to meet their tomorrows. God assures them of his presence; with this companionship, believers can live confidently.

Personal Learning Activities

1. Paul used a favorite term to express his love for and sense of relatedness to other Christians. From the following list,

choose the proper word.

_____ (1) Friends   _____ (3) Saints

_____ (2) Brethren   _____ (4) Christians

2. Match the following lists by pairing the terms with their correct definitions.

_____ (1) Paul

_____ (2) Jerusalem

_____ (3) Claudius Lysias

_____ (4) Caesarea

_____ (5) Sanhedrin

_____ (6) Collection

_____ (7) Felix

_____ (8) Nero

(a) Roman officer who rescued Paul from a Jewish mob

(b) Jewish court before which Paul was tried

(c) Roman emperor before whom Paul waited to be tried

(d) Where Paul was mobbed by Jews

(e) Governor before whom Paul was tried

(f) Took the Gentile churches' offering to the Jerusalem Christians

(g) Gentile churches' aid to the poor saints in Jerusalem

(h) City where Paul was imprisoned for two years before going to Rome

3. Paul viewed his imprisonment as a serious disruption of the spread of the gospel. True _____ False _____

4. Paul wrote that preachers in Rome were proclaiming the gospel out of two motives. Select the correct motives from the following list.

_____ (1) Money   _____ (3) Desire for prestige

_____ (2) Goodwill   _____ (4) Envy and rivalry

5. From the following list, select the proper meanings for the word *salvation*.

_____ (1) The beginning of the new life in Christ

_____ (2) The Christian's present and progressive life

_____ (3) The Christians eternal, blessed hope

Answers:

1. (2); 2. (1) f, (2) d, (3) a, (4) h, (5) b, (6) g, (7) e, (8) c; 3. False; 4. (2), (4); 5. All answers.

47

4

Unity and Steadfastness in Christ

Philippians 1:27 to 2:4

In 1:12-26, Paul had taken the Philippian Christians into his confidence in order that they might share his point of view. In 1:27 to 2:16, he began to appeal to them more directly to demonstrate the spirit and work of mature Christians. He appealed for unity, harmony, obedience, and steadfastness.

Evidently, some discord was present in the church. This discord probably had not reached a critical stage but was in the making. The members were quarreling, and their quarrels troubled Paul.

Paul did not go into detail about the disputes, but he gave several hints about the disunity within the church (1:27; 2:2-3,14; 3:2,18-19; 4:2-3). Evidently these disagreements were resulting in rivalries. One of the reasons Paul wrote the Philippian letter was to deal with these problems.

The section 1:27 to 2:16 falls into three distinct divisions. However, these divisions are connected closely with each other. The doctrinal discussion (2:5-11) forms a link between the two exhortations (1:27 to 2:4 and 2:12-16). All three divisions are directed to the promotion of unity and steadfastness by the practice of self-forgetfulness and obedience. Paul had several grounds for his appeals in 1:27 to 2:16. These include the Philippian Christians' respect for Paul, the impression they made on their unsaved neighbors, their gratitude for being Christian, and the model provided by Christ.

In 1:27 to 2:4, Paul exhorted his readers to unity, steadfastness, and humility. The Philippian Christians were to live well, work together, suffer courageously, and have high regard for one another.

Exhortation to Live Worthy Lives (1:27-30)

The Standard: The Gospel of Christ

Paul's mention in verse 26 of his anticipated visit and its joyful effects led him to write in verse 27, with caution and entreaty, of Christian duty. This duty was the same whether he visited the Philippian Christians or not. Paul's confidence that he would be acquitted and set free fell short of absolute certainty. He was aware of the possibility that he would be condemned and executed. Therefore, he needed to prepare the Philippian Christians for either eventuality. Only one (emphatic in the Greek) admonition was necessary regardless of the trial's outcome. Paul appealed to his readers to have as their one aim to live in a manner "worthy of the gospel of Christ" (v. 27).

The Greek word (*politeuesthe*) rendered "let your manner of life" primarily referred to life in cities or states. What Paul wrote can be translated literally, Perform your duties as citizens worthily of the gospel of Christ.

Philippi was a Roman colony (Acts 16:12), which was one of the most coveted civic prizes of the Roman Empire. A Roman colony was different from anything which we usually mean by the word *colony*. In a Roman colony, the city of Rome was transplanted, as it were, into another part of the Empire. A Roman colony was intended primarily as a military safeguard of a frontier and as a check on insurgent provincials. Like the military highways, the colonies were part of the effective fortification system which kept the Empire safe. They also served as convenient land holdings for rewarding veterans who had served in the wars. The colonists went out with all the pride of Roman citizens to reproduce and represent the city of Rome in the midst of an alien population. Their names still were enrolled in one of the Roman tribes. The insignia of Rome flew over the colony. The Latin language was spoken, and the coins had Latin inscriptions.

Many of the people in Philippi were Roman citizens. Paul was a Roman citizen (Acts 16:37). The word *citizen* was used to describe a person who had the freedom of the city of Rome and could exercise the political and civil privileges of the Roman government. To be a Roman citizen was an honor and a privilege. Paul was writing the Philippian letter from Rome. His presence there and his escape from death in Jerusalem was due to his having exercised his citizenship rights when he appealed to Caesar (Acts 25:6-12). Paul thought of the Philippian Christians as citizens. They were citizens of Rome, but they also were citizens of heaven.

The Greek word *politeuo* developed a wider significance than merely to be a citizen. It was used to refer to membership in a society and to the life-style demanded of all members of the society. Paul seems to have used the word to indicate that the gospel was meant to affect the life-style of the Christians in Philippi. Their business was to act out their citizenship, to prove its reality in their conduct, and to manifest to the world what sort of citizenship it was. They were to live in such a manner as to be "worthy of the gospel of Christ" (v. 27). They constituted a commonwealth presided over by One greater than Caesar, Christ.

Oneness in the Faith

The Philippian Christians' performance of their duties as citizens of heaven was not to depend on Paul's presence. Paul thought that he would be released, and he intended to visit them. However, the possibility existed that he could not come to Philippi. Even if he could not come, he would hear that they stood firm and were bound together in the common fight of faith. Their obligation to live "worthy of the gospel" (v. 27) was independent of the contingency of Paul's circumstances.

In verse 27, Paul used two metaphors to exhort his readers to perform their duties as citizens of heaven. First, he used the metaphor of a soldier and urged the Philippians to "stand firm." This word (*stēkete* in Greek) suggests that the Christians were not to retreat, yield to circumstances, or cower before their enemies. But quietly, resolutely, and determinedly, they were to hold their ground. This word indirectly introduces the situation in the church. Present in the city were the unfriendly attitudes of the Roman law and of public opinion (Acts 16:19-24). Also, the pressure of general unbelief and skepticism was present. Paul entreated the Christians to "stand firm" in their faith, remaining true to the unseen Lord. Not only so, but looking on "the faith" as

the way of affirming the living Christ in their lives, they were to throw themselves into the struggle. No compromise was to be made with evil and error.

Paul used a second metaphor in verse 27 to exhort the Philippian Christians to perform their duties as citizens of heaven. His metaphor was that of an athletic team. His readers were to strive "side by side." The metaphor was drawn from the games; whether the games were racing or wrestling, they involved earnestness and concentration. The believers were to have one fixed, irrevocable purpose with no vacillation, no distraction. They were to encourage and help each other when they stood shoulder to shoulder in the conflict. The Philippian Christians were not to strive with each other but were to promote and defend the cause of Christ.

The Philippian Christians were to "stand firm" and strive "side by side" with "one spirit" and "one mind." The need for

Christian unity, active harmony, was prominent in Paul's thinking when he wrote the Philippian letter.

The unity which Paul desired for his readers did not consist of uniformity of beliefs or opinions, but in identity in a supreme purpose and love. Spirits and minds have only one meeting place, and that is in the object of a great love. Let the union of hearts be complete, and spirits and minds will be united. The indwelling Holy Spirit can direct all the affections to the progress of the gospel. The more fully the Holy Spirit abides in a church, the more the members will be disposed to love one another and to reject party spirit.

Paul wanted the Philippian Christians to understand that they were not isolated individuals, but members of the community of faith, united together in one body. He wanted them to have the same faith in Christ, the same love toward each other, and the same disposition toward the world.

In verse 28, Paul used the metaphor of a startled horse to exhort his readers to perform their duties as citizens of heaven. To be united in spirit was not enough; they also must exhibit an unflinching courage. The Greek word translated "frightened" (pturomenoi, found only here in the New Testament) was used to describe the behavior of a horse when it became scared, sprang aside, or dashed off wildly. It was an expression of panic or dismay. Evidently the opponents of the gospel in Philippi were trying to strike terror into the Christians' hearts and throw them into panic.

That the Philippian Christians were experiencing some form of suffering is evident. Paul admonished them to face the opposition fearlessly. He appealed to them not to be terrified or intimidated by the unexpected appearance of opposition or the sudden attack of an enemy. They were not to waver.

The Christians' fearlessness would impose on their opponents the unwelcome conviction that the opponents were storing up anguish and tribulation for themselves against the day of judgment. The believers' fearlessness also would convince their opponents that they (the enemies of the gospel) were contending against more than human force.

The Christians' fearlessness was from God; it was not a natural characteristic. If their fearlessness had been only a state of mind into which they could enter without divine assistance, it would have proved nothing about salvation. But if such fearlessness was God's gift, then it was evidence of salvation. Paul seemed to suggest that God was working on the hearts and consciences of the opponents with premonitions of their doom and persuasions of the good that awaited the persecuted.

Suffering for Christ

Verse 29 confirms what Paul had just written. "For" in this verse looks back to the "clear omen" in verse 28. Not only is fearlessness a gift of God's grace, but faith and suffering also are privileges opened up for the Christian by God's grace. Paul indicated to his Philippian friends that faith and suffering are twin gifts of God. He said that God, on Christ's behalf, gives his people the privilege not only to believe in him, but also to suffer for him. All who deserve the name Christian are to witness for Christ by their faith. Some witness for Christ by their sufferings.

To Paul, faith was opening life to God through Christ in personal trust and surrender. (See the discussion on Phil. 1:1.) Faith is not content with accepting salvation; it longs to glorify Christ who saves. This qualitative change and this desire to make Christ known brings Christians into painful conflict with the powers of the world (John 16:33). Because believers are united with Christ, they will encounter suffering designed to harm Christ's cause.

Suffering is not a privilege in itself. But suffering "for the sake of Christ" (v. 29) is a grace gift. It brings Christ nearer to the Christian's heart. It also brings the believer an assurance of salvation (John 15:19-21; 1 Pet. 4:14). In addition, suffering for Christ will be rewarded (Rom. 8:18; 2 Cor. 4:17).

Christian fearlessness must come from God because, after enabling a person to trust Christ, he grants the glory of suffering for Christ. To the unbeliever, this is a strange paradox because that person does not want to suffer. But Christian experience proves that the paradox is true (Acts 5:41; Rom. 5:3; Col. 1:24). The prospect of suffering could have terrified the Philippian Christians. But Paul indicated that if they viewed it in God's light, they would discover that suffering for the gospel's sake was a gift of God's grace.

In verse 30, Paul reminded the Philippian Christians that they were standing on common ground with him. He knew that they regarded his struggles for the gospel as something extraordinary. They esteemed him as a great apostle on whom much depended. In contrast, their experience of conflict with evil seemed insignificant. Paul would not allow them to think in this way.

Paul wanted his readers to know that the fight of faith is common to all Christians. In nature and essence, Christians share the same struggle.

Exhortation to Respect One Another (2:1-4)

Motivations for Unity

In 2:1, Paul appealed to his readers by all their deepest experiences as Christians to preserve unity and peace. He used a fourfold appeal to stress the motive for the unity he enjoined in verse 2. The connecting word "so" or therefore refers to the duty of having "one mind" which was enjoined in 1:27 and is urged again in 2:2. Apparently a double threat was posed to the unity and harmony of the Philippian church: false teachers (3:1-3) and disagreeing members (4:1-3). The discord could not have been pronounced because Paul did not warn or rebuke them. However, the lack of unity was real.

With great earnestness, Paul appealed to his readers to be of the "same mind" (v. 2). He wanted them to cultivate a disposition that would produce unity and harmony among the membership. Paul was aware that a great difference exists between unity and uniformity. He knew that true spiritual unity must come from within and that uniformity is the result of pressure from without. That was the reason Paul began the paragraph (2:1-4) by appealing to the highest spiritual motives. Paul stated the appeal forcefully by a fourfold repetition of "any" and by listing four articles of faith and matters of Christian experience which were self-evident to the readers. The "if" (v. 1) did not express uncertainty. Rather it meant, in view of the fact. It was intended to fix the readers' thoughts on the various grounds of Paul's appeal.

The first Christian experience to which Paul appealed for unity was "encouragement in Christ" (v. 1). The Greek word translated "encouragement" (*paraklēsis*) also can be translated comfort, consolation, and exhortation.

If the believers had Christ's Spirit in their lives—and Paul assumed that they had—they would have a strong bond of unity. Christ's life is in the life of each Christian, and that life is diffused through all the members of the church. The life of the vine is present in each branch (John 15:1-16). If the church's spiritual life is one, then unity aids its growth and discord checks its growth.

The Christian is an individual and a social being, and his or her normal social condition is unity. The church is one body (Eph. 2:16; 4:4), and all Christians are members of it. All the members are animated by one life, and each contributes to the good of the whole. Thus unity is the ideal; but selfishness, egotism, and pride in the believers create division.

The second Christian experience to which Paul appealed for unity was the "incentive of love" (v. 1). This was an appeal to the readers' experience of Christ's love in their sufferings. The Greek word translated "incentive" also may be translated consolation. The Greek word translated "love" (agapēs) means unconquerable goodwill toward others. It is not a mere reaction of the heart; it is a victory of the will achieved by Christ's help. It is the subjective result of the objective reality of Christ's presence in the believer's life. This selfless love would provide the Philippian Christians with the incentive for unity.

The third Christian experience to which Paul appealed for unity was "participation in the Spirit" (v. 1). The Greek word translated "participation" (koinōnia) also means communion, sharing, fellowship, and partnership. The precise meaning of "participation in the Spirit" is not certain. The phrase may mean the unity of feeling that is produced by the Holy Spirit. It also can mean the joint participation of all believers in the Spirit. But, practically, the two meanings coincide. The Holy Spirit, in whom all Christians participate in varying degrees, shares his gifts and graces (Gal. 5:22-23) which are the basis of all true unity. The Spirit's presence in each Christian constitutes the church's inner unity. Since the Philippian Christians were partakers of a common life in the Holy Spirit, Paul appealed to them to make the promotion of the common life their aim.

The fourth Christian experience to which Paul appealed for unity was "affection and sympathy." (See 1:8 for a discussion on "affection.") The Greek term translated "sympathy," oiktirmoi, is literally compassions, kindnesses. The singular noun can mean mercy or grace. These two words emphasize emotions which flow from one life common to all believers.

Paul had indicated that he derived joy from the Philippian Christians' life and conduct (1:4-5). In verse 2, he entreated them to complete his joy by living in unity. A greater spirit of oneness, humility, and helpfulness on their part could supply what still was lacking in his joy. The injunction in verse 2 is drawn from the four experiences given in verse 1. Paul asserted that if these four experiences were real in his readers' lives, then unity in the church should follow as a natural consequence.

The main injunction in verse 2 is that the believers be "of the same mind." This main injunction is followed by three appeals which are nearly synonymous with the main command: "having the same love, being in full accord and of one mind." The unity which Paul desired for his readers was far deeper and more vital than mere agreement of opinion, or sameness of policy, or cooperation in practice. What he desired was unity produced in the lives of those who had their hearts directed to Christ, who could make them one.

The Need for Selflessness

The Greek text of verse 3 has no verb before the word "nothing"; therefore, a verb needs to be supplied. To supply a verb from the preceding exhortation may be best: the translation would be: Contemplate ("one mind," v. 2) nothing. . . . Paul wrote that nothing must be done or contemplated from "selfishness or conceit" (v. 3).

The word translated "selfishness" in verse 3 is the same word that is translated "partisanship" in 1:17. It sometimes is translated contention and faction. It was a word used to describe a partisan spirit which engendered strife.

"Selfishness" is an undue regard for one's interests regardless of others' interests. It is the essential principle of sin in the sense that it is the assertion of one's will as opposed to submission to God's will.

The Greek word translated "conceit" sometimes is translated vainglory. In this form, it is found nowhere else in the New Testament. This word denotes boastful pride; it describes the spirit which makes great claims for self and disparages others. The basic idea seems to be a desire to honor oneself.

Paul urged the Philippian Christians not to do anything merely as the result of selfishness and conceit. They were not to form a faction or party in the church. This command prohibited them from doing anything as the result of strife. Selfishness and conceit were not principles from which they were to act or by which they were to be governed. They were to form no plan and aim at no object on the basis of selfishness. Christians are factious when they are concerned (1) to establish their opinions rather than the truth, (2) to advance their party rather than the gospel of Christ, (3) to add to their importance rather than to preserve the peace of the church.

The solution to the problem of selfishness and conceit is the practice of "humility" (v. 3). The word translated "humility" appears to have been coined by the New Testament writers. This word denotes a spiritual grace. It is the opposite of selfishness which leads people to strive for ascendancy or to act for flattery. Humility indicates a self-forgetfulness which enables one to form a right view of others. The early Christians used the word to signify the spirit which most resembled that of Christ. Paul directed the Philippian Christians to look at their personal faults and at the good points in the lives of their fellow-Christians as a discipline of humility. This was to be done not only outwardly but by true humility when each, through self-denial, turned his or her thoughts away from self and toward others.

Humble people do not think disparagingly of themselves. They know themselves, and they accept themselves. At the same time, they keep themselves under judgment. Humble people know that they have inward, deep defects and failings which are unknown to their fellow-Christians and which they have no right to suppose that others have. On the other hand, humble persons see in others virtues which they know that they do not possess.

In verse 4, Paul concluded his exhortation by adding, "Let each of you look not only to his own interests, but also to the interests of others." This was a personal appeal. Paul had implied that as long as he knew of disunity in the church which was so dear to him, he could not be completely happy (Phil. 2:2). If his readers would complete his joy, they must complete their fellowship.

In the Greek text, no period is placed at the end of verse 3; the sentence continues, and the opening phrase of verse 4 should be translated: not looking. The Greek word translated "interests" is indefinite. It can be translated as things, possessions, rights, qualities, ideas, or gifts. Perhaps Paul left it indefinite so that it would speak to any situation where Christians were obsessed with themselves. The situation in the church seems to have been one in which individual members claimed high positions for themselves as a right.

Paul's obvious intention in verse 4 was to encourage the Philippian Christians to have real humility and unselfishness. He did not suggest that anyone was claiming honors that were undeserved. The point he made was that they should not insist on receiving even the honors that they deserved. The Christian spirit is renunciation, not self-assertion; it is concern for others, not concern for self and one's rights.

The injunctions do not mean that Christians are to neglect their interests. For them to look to their interests is not wrong; to look to them exclusively *is* wrong. Every person, including Christians, has interests to which he or she must attend. These include physical health, intellectual growth, material resources. However, the precept means that Christians are not to attend to their interests chiefly and in such a way as to neglect others' interests. No real conflict exists between the interests of self and the interests of others. We can secure our happiness or well-being only by promoting the interests of others. The law of love regulates Christian conduct and carries Christians out of the narrow circle of personal interest into the broader one of common welfare.

Paul's exhortation reiterates Jesus' command: "Love one another" (John 15:12). No other command can be obeyed without this one (Rom. 13:10). The Christian cannot love God without this love, and this is "pure and undefiled" religion (Jas. 1:27).

Christians secure a life of real liberty when they look no longer only on their interests but also have an eye for those of others. Frank Stagg summed it up:

> The only rivalry which is proper in Christians is that in which each seeks to outdo the other in esteeming the other. One is not to be concerned about receiving honors or advantages for himself. He is to be concerned that his brethren be honored and served.[1]

Lessons for Life from the Scriptures

Christians must answer to the demand that they live in a manner worthy of the gospel. The good news is that salvation is God's gift to those who will receive it. Each person can experience grace that redeems and sustains. The demand of grace is that believers live up to the highest standards that God has revealed in Christ. Anything less is unworthy of the gospel.

Living in a manner worthy of the gospel means, at least in part, that the Christian contributes to the unity of God's people. All Christians are not alike and are not to seek to become alike. Each believer is a unique personality. But when Christ's redemptive work is given priority in each life, churches experience a unity of spirit and purpose that allows Christ to use those fellowships effectively. A party spirit fragments any local expression of the body of Christ; power struggles in a church mean a powerless church. Oneness in spirit and purpose allows Christ to empower his people.

Living in a manner worthy of the gospel means that Christians maintain a healthy respect for, and genuine interest in, one another. If Christians fail to exhibit God's kind of love toward one another, they cannot extend it to others who need redeeming love. To fail at the point of love is to fail at our most crucial point of responsibility toward each other. Loveless Christianity is a grotesque contradiction.

---

1. *The Broadman Bible Commentary*, Vol. 11 (Nashville: Broadman Press, 1971), p. 194.

Personal Learning Activities

1. The Philippian church was the only one of Paul's churches that had no discord, no fellowship problems. True _____ False _____
2. In 1:27-28, Paul used three metaphors to exhort his readers to perform their duties as citizens of heaven. From the following list, select those metaphors.
   _____ (1) A soldier   _____ (3) An athletic team
   _____ (2) A government   _____ (4) A startled horse
3. The unity Paul desired for his readers was uniformity of beliefs. True _____ False _____
4. To Paul, _____ and _____ were twin gifts of God. (Select the correct answers from the following list.)
   (1) Faith   (3) Suffering
   (2) Success   (4) Prosperity
5. Love (*agapē*) may be defined as unconquerable goodwill toward others. True _____ False _____

Answers:
1. False; 2. (1), (3), (4); 3. False; 4. (1), (3); 5. True.

59

5

The Mind of Christ

Philippians 2:5-16

In 2:5-11, Paul enforced his exhortation to unity, steadfastness, and humility by Christ's example. The wonderful descent of Christ to meet people's need, failure, shame, and sorrow was given that it might be a living inspiration and example for Christians. Believers are not to look on their interests only, but are to be willing to stoop for others in need, failure, shame, and sorrow. As God worked through Christ to accomplish redemption, God can work through his people to accomplish his purpose. And his purpose is that people be won to his grace and that Christians "grow in the grace and knowledge of our Lord and Savior Jesus Christ" (2 Pet. 3:18). The passage 2:5-11, the only doctrinal one in Philippians, is one of the most important Christological statements in the New Testament.

That the short passage—2:5-11—occurs in such an incidental manner is remarkable. Paul did not write to define Christological doctrine. He wrote to stimulate and encourage the Philippian Christians by Christ's example of humility and self-giving. He also wrote to settle disputes about honor and positions among the church members. Moreover, Paul did not conceive of Christlikeness as being produced in Christians by imitation. By "this mind" (v. 5), he did not mean Christ's intellect; he meant Christ's attitude toward God's will and toward people. Christ is the perfect example of how Christians should act. He is an example of humility and self-sacrifice with a view to the welfare of others.

Christ's attitude toward God and toward people was one of

self-giving at whatever cost. The proof of his attitude was his incarnation, lowly service, and death. God would produce the same attitude in the Philippian Christians. Their responsibility was to let him do it.

Paul's appeal was that the attitude which governed Christ also govern the church. The passage 2:5-11 arises out of that which precedes, and it prepares the way for what follows. Paul called his readers to enter the mind of Christ, not out of curiosity but for the reformation of their lives. The establishment of harmonious thought and action required that each member repress self-assertion and renounce much that might be claimed as rights. Christ's life was a unique pattern of such humility.

The Example of Christ (2:5-11)

Christ's Equality with God

Verse 5 is abbreviated in the Greek text. Literally it is: This think in yourselves which [was?] also in Christ Jesus. Some interpreters think that Paul was using the example of Christ in terms of Christ's inmost self or mind. That is, the Philippian Christians were to adopt Christ's way of thinking or disposition. This is a possible interpretation. Other interpreters think that Paul was using the example of Christ to appeal to the church to have Christ's mind in their community of faith—"among yourselves." That is, in their relationships with each other, believers were to exhibit the "mind" they already had as persons in Christ. This also is a possible interpretation. Probably, Paul included both ideas in his statement.

The imitation of Christ does not consist in trying to imagine and do the things which Christ would do. It consists in seeking to cultivate the spirit and the disposition which Christ possessed and practiced. By "mind" Paul meant Christ's attitude, moral temper, and way of thinking. Paul meant particularly Christ's humble, unselfish devotion.

To appeal to the Philippian Christians, Paul used the example of Christ's utter humility in subjecting himself to God in perfect obedience. Christ's followers were to emulate Christ's "mind."

Probably, no other passage in the New Testament has given rise to more discussion than verse 6. Nearly every word that Paul wrote had several usages. One of the major problems in interpreting this verse has to do with time. Did Paul refer to Christ's preincarnate state or did he refer to Christ's life on earth? Interpreters disagree.

Paul began with the phrase "who, though he was in the form of God." Many interpreters think that Paul referred to the preexistence of Christ. The New Testament teaches that Christ existed before he was born in Bethlehem. In John's Gospel, the writer began: "In the beginning was the Word, and the Word was with God, and the Word was God. . . . And the Word became flesh and dwelt among us" (John 1:1,14*a*). Christ's preexistence is reflected in his teaching (John 8:58). Preexistence also is indicated in Jesus' last prayer (John 17:5). Paul alluded to Christ's preexistence in his earlier writings (1 Cor. 8:6; 2 Cor. 8:9). Paul could have meant that Christ consented to leave his preexistent, heavenly state for the earthly one.

However, many interpreters think that the phrase "who, though he was in the form of God" refers to Jesus' earthly existence. Some of these interpreters see a reflection of the typology in which Christ is the second Adam. Unlike the first Adam who wanted to be like God (Gen. 3:5), the second Adam wanted to obey and serve God.[1] The New Testament writers saw Christ as God and also as a man (John 1:1; Acts 2:22; 1 Tim. 2:5). Christianity centers around a real man, a human being, a historical person.

Obviously, Christ was preexistent and also was meek and lowly in heart during his life on earth (Matt. 11:29). To which did Paul refer in this verse? Since he was not discussing theology or speculating on Christ's nature, he probably was referring to Christ's life while he was on earth. Paul was dealing with the problem of dissension in the Philippian church. He used the supreme example of Christ's unselfishness and voluntary humiliation to challenge the Philippian Christians to act as Christ had acted.

The Greek word for "form" occurs three times in the New Testament (Mark 16:12; Phil. 2:6-7). The word connotes reality along with appearance. It implies much more than an apparent resemblance. It refers to the inner, essential, and abiding nature of a person or thing. Paul used the term in verse 6 to indicate that Christ was God. He possessed the same kind of existence as God possesses; he was God in his nature, essence, and being. Christ inwardly possessed the divine nature and outwardly displayed the divine glory. Only God can be in the "form of God." Persons were made in the image of God, but persons are not in the "form of God." Paul expressed the truth in this way because he wished to make the reference to Christ's godhood balance the reference to his servanthood (v. 7). Since Paul preferred not to write that Christ became a servant, he wrote that Christ took "the form of a servant" (v. 7). Therefore, Paul wrote that Christ "was in the form of God" (v. 6). To express in human speech more explicitly Christ's divinity would be difficult.

Though Christ was the God-Man, he did not regard equality with God a treasure to be gripped strongly and retained at all risks. The word "grasped" (v. 6) is found only here in the New Testament. Christ possessed the treasure, but he resolved not to cling to it. For the sake of people, he was willing to surrender his prerogatives and powers which rightfully belong to him. This was the supreme example of one's refusing to look only to his interests. He "came not to be served but to serve" (Mark 10:45).

Christ's Self-Emptying

Instead of holding on to his equality with God, Christ "emptied himself, taking the form of a servant, being born in the likeness of men" (v. 7). When did Christ empty himself? Probably, Paul meant that the emptying took place all along during the incarnation. As a man, Christ subjected himself to God's authority and to God's providence. As a man, he entered a discipline of obedience. He used his equality with God as an opportunity, not to exalt himself but to abase himself. He renounced all his glorious prerogatives and became a servant.

The essential idea in the word "emptied" (v. 7) is that of bringing to vanity or nothingness. The word was used to describe a person who laid aside rank, prestige, and dignity to become as nothing in respect to these. The word was used to describe a person who assumed a more humble position and station than he or she really deserved.

The phrase "the form of a servant" (v. 7) indicates the condition of a servant as distinguished from one of higher rank. It means to appear as a servant, to perform the work of a servant, and to be regarded as a servant. Christ was made like a servant in the lowly condition which he assumed in his redemptive mission. The language implies that Christ took a humble place. He laid aside that which expressed his divine being and took on the form of a servant. He came to serve. He did not look primarily to his interests. Paul's object was to state the depth of humiliation to which Christ descended. Paul emphasized this by stating that Christ descended to the lowest condition of humanity (Luke

22:27; John 13:4-15).

Christ was "born in the likeness of men" (v. 7). His outward appearance was altogether human. He really was *like* men, as he truly *was* a man. However, he was more than a man; he was the God-Man. Without this fact, he would have had no resemblance to humanity, only identity. The fact that he was the God-Man did not prevent him from accepting the conditions involved in a truly human life, with the liabilities to trial, misunderstanding, and suffering. Karl Barth wrote: "What we see is man, the form of one exposed to all the dubiousness, ambiguity, and darkness of an individual human existence, the form not of a lord but of a servant."[2] Christ never used his deity for his benefit. He lived as a man.

Christ accepted the true position of a man, which is obedience. The true person—the authentic person—cannot live any life other than that of obedience and service. Christ laid aside his divine power that he might receive power from God. In this way, he lived a truly human life.

Christ's Humility

In verse 8, Paul described the deepest level in Christ's emptying process. The words "being found in human form" describe Christ's true manhood. The phrase indicates how he was perceived and recognized by his contemporaries. He was recognized as a human being. The fact that he was more than a man molds the expression into this familiar form. If the eyes of his contemporaries had been opened, they would have realized that those who had seen Christ had seen the Father (John 14:9). However, Christ's manifestation to the world was in all the weakness of humanity.

Paul wrote that Christ willingly accepted the human conditions of powerlessness and mortality. Christ took on the attributes and was open to the infirmities of the human condition. He became human. He needed food, rest, and clothing. He was liable to suffering and death.

As the God-Man, Christ could display God's moral glory through his human nature. However, he did not assume and assert the prerogatives of deity. He did not demand the service of others, but he condescended to the lowest conditions of life. He did not display fully his glorious rank and divine powers.

Christ truly was God, and he truly was a man. As a man, "he humbled himself" (v. 8). As a man, he did not assume some

pinnacle of the human scene; he willingly surrendered his internal superiority of gifts and powers. Instead of commanding and ruling in power and majesty, he allowed himself to be humiliated and abused. His place was not one of honor, authority, and preeminence among people. From the manger to the cross, he walked a path of humiliation.

Christ's life-long humbling of himself was manifested further in his becoming "obedient" (v. 8). Paul did not indicate here to whom the obedience was rendered. However, that he meant obedience to God is quite certain. Christ placed himself in the condition of a servant to do God's will, and he never shrank from what that condition involved. He subjected himself to God and obeyed him completely (Matt. 26:39; John 5:30). Christ maintained this obedience and submission to God's will to the end.

Christ's obedience to God extended through every detail of his life. He said, "I have come down from heaven, not to do my own will, but the will of him who sent me" (John 6:38). The author of Hebrews wrote that Christ's doing God's will ended in the offering of Christ's body (Heb. 10:9-10). The supreme act of obedience was Christ's voluntary submission to death. His death was in obedience to God, because by it he carried out the Father's will for the salvation of the world. Jesus Christ never was seen more plainly to be God than when he gave up his life as a man.

Christ was obedient to the extent that he voluntarily submitted to death—death in its most ignominious and painful form. Crucifixion was the most torturous, shameful, and degrading death in the ancient world. Christ submitted to death on a cross, in public, in agony, without dignity—death which seemed to proclaim aloud the triumph and power of death. He died the long, lingering, painful, humiliating death of the cross. A curse was attached to anyone who suffered this mode of death (Deut. 21:23; Gal. 3:13). A greater contrast than Jesus' death on the cross never occurred: omnipotence and seeming helplessness; the throne in glory and the cross! Here is obedience and self-abnegation which essentially is the Christ spirit.

Paul did not say that God willed Christ's death on the cross. No New Testament writer indicated that God wanted or needed Jesus to be crucified. Christ obeyed God in giving his life—to whatever extent necessary for redemption—in accord with the Father's will (Gal. 1:3-4). The Father willed that Jesus offer to share himself completely with people. The New Testament writers indicated only two reasons for Jesus' death: people's sin and God's love. God loved persons so much that he offered himself to them in Jesus Christ. Paul wrote: "In Christ God was reconciling the world to himself" (2 Cor. 5:19). In Peter's sermon at Pentecost, he said that Jesus was "delivered up according to the definite plan and foreknowledge of God" (Acts 2:23). God's plan was that Jesus be "delivered up" or to offer himself to people; he did not will that they crucify Jesus. In the same sermon at Pentecost, Peter said that lawless men "crucified and killed" Jesus (Acts 2:23). God loved persons and gave Jesus to save them (John 3:16); people rejected, betrayed, and murdered him (Acts 7:52).

In 2:5-8, Paul gave the program of the "mind" of Christ; in 2:9-11, he indicated the reaction of God. "Therefore" (v. 9) implies that God responded to Christ's obedience and humiliation in accordance with a dynamic principle: Those who humble themselves will be exalted (Matt. 23:12; Jas. 4:6). Christ humbled himself, and God exalted him.

Christ's Exaltation

The characteristics of Christ's life were humility, obedience, and self-denial. Christ did not try to coerce or manipulate others; he only desired to serve others. He did not want his way; he wanted God's way. He did not attempt to exalt himself; he only tried to bless others. As a consequence of Christ's humility and obedience, God "highly exalted him" (v. 9).

The Greek text has the conjunction "also" as the second word of verse 9 (literally, therefore also). The conjunction goes with all that follows and connects Christ's life of humiliation with God's act of exaltation. God set his seal on Christ's self-sacrifice and obedience by exalting him and giving him "the name which is above every name" (v. 9).

Paul did not say what the name was, but from what follows he seems to have meant that God gave Christ his name—"Lord" (v. 11). At the crucifixion, Christ reached the lowest level a human being could reach. Yet, this same Christ is Lord and God. He did not displace God; he is God, and his life, death, and resurrection are God's works.

The Christ who was denied, betrayed, rejected, and crucified is now the exalted Lord. In the name Lord are focused his authority, power, dignity, honor, dominion, and worthiness of adoration. The word Lord is used in the Septuagint (the Old Testament in Greek) to translate the name for God—Jehovah or Yahweh.

In ancient thought, a name was not merely a designation to distinguish one person from another but was an index of character or status. Therefore, the name Lord for Christ declares his true character and dignity (Eph. 1:21).

Paul set forth Jesus' name as being the ground and object of worship when he declared that "at the name of Jesus every knee should bow" (v. 10). These words were quoted from Isaiah 45:23 where they occur in one of the most solemn utterances of Old Testament monotheism. Paul meant that Christ is offered the honor and worship that is proper only to God because Christ bears the name of God—Lord. Christ is one through whom God can be known and worshiped. The phrase "every knee should bow" is a figurative description of homage, respect, adoration, and worship. (See Eph. 3:14.) This phrase means that Christ was so exalted by God that for all in the universe to worship him would be proper. The phrase "in heaven and on earth and under the earth" (v. 10) was Paul's way of indicating the universe.

Paul wrote that a universal expression of silent homage would be given in the bowing of the knees. Also, all created things would give a universal expression of audible worship. All living creatures will acknowledge that "Jesus Christ is Lord" (v. 11). The acknowledgment that Christ is Lord is the acknowledgment of the Father's glory. God is manifested perfectly in Christ. (See John 1:18). Christ's exalted position does not detract from God's glory but rather enhances it. The honor paid to Christ glorifies the Father.

Paul began the paragraph 2:5-11 with the injunction, "Have this mind among yourselves, which is yours in Christ Jesus" (v. 5). How could his readers cling to their pride and ambitions, and how could they persist in their petty quarrels, if they had the mind of Christ and confessed Jesus Christ as Lord? God would give unity to the Philippian Christians when they had the mind of Christ. Through Paul, God was calling the Philippian church to empty itself, to take the form of a servant, and to be obedient in self-giving to the end.

Exhortation to Work Out Salvation (2:12-16)

In 2:5-11, Paul presented Christ as the great example of the humble, obedient mind. Then he pressed home the lesson of Christ's humiliation and obedience. The theological statement about Christ's self-abnegation was not continued beyond the point at which it served Paul's purpose. He only cited Christ's example to challenge the Christians in Philippi to unity in spirit and self-giving service.

Under the stimulus of Christ's example, the Philippian Christians were exhorted to work to achieve the full and complete salvation to which God was inspiring them. The main idea in 2:12-16 is that God lived in the believers and worked out through them the kind of attitudes and activities that Christ demonstrated. Because God was in them, Paul admonished them to manifest Christ's mind amid their ungodly surroundings. Their triumph in this struggle against evil would be Paul's crown in the day of Christ. Even if Paul's life were poured out as a libation with the offering of their faith, that event would be a greater cause for their mutual congratulations and joy.

God's Working in Believers
The word "therefore" in verse 12 connects the exhortation in 2:12-16 with Christ's example (2:15-11). For the first time in the letter, Paul addressed his readers as "beloved." This indicated his deep feeling for them.

Paul encouraged his readers by acknowledging their obedience. He urged them to work, not to approve themselves to him, but for the sake of Christ. They were to realize Christ's presence, and all the more in Paul's absence. They always had obeyed God, both when Paul was present and when he was absent. Their obedience to God was not to depend on Paul's presence. The verb "obeyed" does not have an object, but evidently Paul meant obedience to God.

Paul's exhortation meant for the Philippian Christians to rely on God's Spirit in them rather than on Paul. To depend too much on Paul was to doubt God's guidance.

The Greek verb translated "work out" (v. 12) means to bring to full completion, to full accomplishment and conclusion. It was used to refer to an act of carrying out to completion that which already had been started. The Philippian Christians were to "work out" their "own salvation." This admonition did not suggest that they were to work for or toward their salvation. Paul was not referring to a salvation which would become theirs if they worked for it, but to a salvation which they already enjoyed. They were not to work it into their lives; they were to work it out of their lives in daily behavior.

The Philippian Christians already possessed salvation. They had opened their lives to God through faith in Christ; God had shared his life with them through the Holy Spirit. The change which God had made in their lives was not complete. God still was working in them to complete the Christlike life (Eph. 4:13). However, he was not working apart from them. The Holy Spirit is free, and he respects persons' moral freedom. He does not compel or coerce. He preserves moral freedom; he does not supersede the moral and spiritual faculties but qualifies and changes these faculties by his indwelling presence.

The word "salvation" is used in the New Testament with several shades of meaning; most of the usages include the ideas of rescuing and healing. The word sometimes expresses a Christian's whole experience in Christ. At other times, it is used to refer to one of three phases of life in Christ. Salvation has a beginning, a progress, and an end. The word may denote deliverance from the results and presence of sin. In verse 12, Paul used the word "salvation" to refer to deliverance from the power of sin.

The Philippian Christians' salvation was a personal matter; it was their own salvation. Each one was to work out salvation for himself or herself. Each one stood in an individual relationship to Christ. The Philippian Christians were warned to work out their salvation "with fear and trembling" (v. 12). This phrase was quite common with Paul (1 Cor. 2:3; 2 Cor. 7:15; Eph. 6:5), and he was the only New Testament writer to use it. These words do not mean cowardly or slavish fright, but reverence and submission to God. Paul's readers were to be aware that (1) God was the one with whom they had to deal, (2) they were constantly in his presence, and (3) he was acting effectively among them and within them. Christians must be conscious of their weakness and continual moral peril. They also must be conscious of God's presence in their lives and in the church's life.

Verse 13 gives the reason why the Philippian Christians were to work out their salvation with fear and trembling. God was working in them. Before their conversion, he had worked *on* them by his Spirit; now he was working *in* them through his Spirit. They were to interpret their good impulses and desires to minister as tokens of God's presence and inspiration in their lives. The fact that God was working in them was to be an incentive to their activity.

Every deliberate action has two aspects. One is the hidden aspect of choice. Out of the many live options in a given situation, one must be selected. The mind must decide. The other aspect of every deliberate action is to carry into effect what has been decided. Paul told the Philippian Christians that their hearts' good inclinations and their wills' beneficial purposes were of God.

Paul declared that the motive for the divine indwelling was "for his [God's] good pleasure" (v. 13). God's "good pleasure" is neither that his creatures exist in a corrupted condition nor that they exist in an immature spiritual condition. His "good pleasure" is that the lost be saved (2 Pet. 3:9) and that the saved become Christlike (Eph. 4:13).

The two statements, "Work out your own salvation" (v. 12) and "God is at work in you, both to will and to work" (v. 13), give the two great realities of human freedom and divine sovereignty. Paul seemed to have stated two absolutes. The command to work implies freedom, responsibility, and duty; the divine operation is described as ultimate. Logic dictates one absolute. However, experience transcends logic at many points. In experience, God is sovereign; people are free.

Christians in a Hostile Environment
Paul had written of the necessity of obedience in working out salvation (v. 12). But obedience may be either grudging or voluntary. Hence, Paul continued his exhortation with the admonition: "Do all things without grumbling or questioning" (v. 14). The precept is a broad generality, probably because Paul in-

tended it to be applied both to his readers' relationships with each other and with God. The precept stands in close connection with what has been stated previously. In fact, it is an explanation of how salvation is to be worked out. The admonition presents the human side which corresponds to the divine working on which Paul had insisted.

The word "all" is emphatic and included all the details of the Philippian Christians' daily life. The word "grumbling" (v. 14) was used to describe outward wranglings or discontent, proceeding not so much from the mind as from the heart. According to Barclay, the word "describes the low, threatening, discontented muttering of a mob who distrust their leaders, and who are on the verge of a rebellion and an uprising against them."[3] The word "questioning," according to Barclay, "describes useless, and sometimes ill-natured, disputing and debating, and doubting and wavering."[4] The two words "grumbling" and "questioning," along with the context, seem to indicate that when he wrote verse 14, Paul had in mind Israel's unrest and rebellious utterances against Moses. (See Ex. 15:24; 16:2; Num. 16:41; 1 Cor. 10:10.) The whole discussion centered on the danger to the Philippian Christians' faith of being disunited.

In verse 14, Paul seemed to compare the Christian life to a pilgrimage, like the Hebrews' journey from slavery in Egypt to the Promised Land. However, he told his Philippian friends that they should not imitate the Hebrews in the Hebrews' constant grumbling and questioning. All the dictates of God's will were to be obeyed cheerfully. This precept recalls Paul's previous admonitions for harmony and unity.

In verse 15, Paul continued to show how his readers were to work out their salvation. They were exhorted to exhibit in their lives a contrast to the behavior of the rebellious Israelites. Believers were to become examples to the world of high Christian living. They were to exemplify a spirit and maintain a life that would guard them from the rebukes of their severest critics. Their lives were to be marked by purity, loftiness, and consistency which would disarm the world's censure. Christians were to be marked not by a mere absence of fault, but by a conspicuous exhibition of all the graces that are identified with the indwelling Holy Spirit.

The phrase "that you may be" (v. 15) would be translated better, that you may become. It is an exhortation to continued progress. The word "blameless" relates to the judgment of others. The Philippian Christians were to give the world no ground for criticism. The word "innocent" sometimes is translated harmless. The Greek implies that which is pure, unmixed, or unalloyed. The word describes a person's intrinsic worth. Paul exhorted his readers to avoid any inconsistency which the world could scorn.

The phrase "children of God" (v. 15) refers primarily to the Philippian Christians' resembling God and thus being recognized as belonging to him. They were partakers of God's life. The "children of God" were to appear "without blemish in the midst of a crooked and perverse generation."

Believers were to shine as "lights" (v. 15) in a dark and perverse world. To translate the Greek word for "lights" as luminaries would be better. The Septuagint (the Old Testament in Greek) uses this word for the sun, moon, and stars (Gen. 1:14, 16). The only other use of the word in the New Testament is in Revelation 21:11.

Christians are those who have been illumined so that saving light radiates from them. To be light without showing it is not possible. Light will shine. Christians are persons who, because they feel God's love, compassion, and grace in their hearts, live lives of joy, love, and service. The more of "the light of the world" (John 8:12) is in the Christian, the better luminary (light) the believer becomes.

Paul told the Philippian Christians that they were to "shine as lights in the world" (v. 15). The "world," as distinguished from the church, is "crooked and perverse." The "world" is the sphere under Satan's domination. "World" therefore is an inclusive term for all those who are in the kingdom of darkness and are not begotten of God.

The world and the church are in sharp contrast to each other; they are two separate, distinct groups of people. Christians are chosen out of the world (John 17:6) and no longer belong to it. They still are "in the world" (John 17:11,15), yet they are distinct from it so that the church and the world are set over against each other (1 John 3:13; John 15:18-19; 17:14). Though the world hates Christians, Christians are not to hate the world. Christians are not to be conformed to, or contaminated by, the world. They are not to escape from the world; they are to remain in it. Paul told the Philippian Christians that they were "lights" (v. 15) shining in the darkness of Philippi.

Paul seemed to keep before him "the day of Christ" (v. 16)

when he would be called on to give the final account of the task entrusted to him. If the Philippian Christians were faithful, he would be able to point to them as his pride, the demonstration that he had not run or labored in vain.

The Greek word translated "holding fast" (v. 16) also can be translated holding forth. That Paul intended both of these ideas is possible, for both were needed. His readers needed to persist in their loyalty and obedience to the word of God. They also needed to hold forth the light of the gospel to the perverse generation. Christianity is life. It cannot be expressed completely in words; to be seen, it must be lived. Jesus pointed to good works as the strongest reason for people to glorify the Father (Matt. 5:16). The gospel's proclamation of freedom from sin is preached and proved best by evidence that Christians are free.

The Philippian Christians were to shine in the dark world by "holding fast the word of life" (v. 16). They were to reveal not merely a moral contrast to the world, but they were to bear witness to Christ from whom all true life comes.

Lessons for Life from the Scriptures

Christians are called to a servant role in our world. Repeatedly, Christ indicated to his disciples that true greatness—greatness that matters—is to be found in service to people. He saw himself as a servant. Paul grasped this concept and pointed to Christ's servanthood as the model for believers. Many people have difficulty with the concept of servanthood as a way of life. Ours is a power-oriented society that places premiums on honors, prestige, influence, station. To many, the cross is an archaic, romanticized symbol whose message of self-giving sounds good but is not allowed to affect life-styles too drastically. We can deny the truth, but we cannot change it: Christ's people are called to minister to people in his spirit.

Christ is exalted when his people give evidence of taking on his character. God has exalted Christ and has given him the superlative name. We bow at the name of Jesus and confess that he is Lord, not in posture and in pious repetition and inflection of the title Lord Jesus Christ, but in our lives' taking on more of his outlook. Christ is exalted when he is obeyed and followed in our daily living.

Each day given to Christians is a day for them to work out their salvation. We have opportunities that allow God's working in us to be expressed by our encouraging, affirming, and giving cups of cold water to others. To incarnate more of Christ's love, mercy, kindness, and acceptance is for us to be busy working out our salvation.

1. See Frank Stagg, "Philippians," *The Broadman Bible Commentary*, Vol. 11 (Nashville: Broadman Press, 1971), p. 196.
2. Karl Barth, *The Epistle to the Philippians* (Richmond: John Knox Press, 1962), p. 64.
3. William Barclay, *The Letters to the Philippians, Colossians, and Thessalonians* (Philadelphia: The Westminster Press, 1959), p. 54.
4. *Ibid.*

Personal Learning Activities

1. To Paul, _____ was the supreme example of humility and self-giving.
2. By the mind of Christ, Paul meant Christ's intellect. True _____ False _____
3. According to Ray Robbins, Christ's self-emptying took place (select the correct answer):
   _____ (1) At the incarnation (birth)
   _____ (2) All along during Christ's life and ministry
   _____ (3) In Gethsemane
   _____ (4) On the cross
4. Christ, in his life and work, took the role of a _____ . (From the following list, choose the proper answer.)
       (1) Servant   (3) Religious leader
       (2) King   (4) Military leader
5. In Philippians 2, Paul wrote that through life and in death, _____ was one of Christ's dominant characteristics. (Choose the proper response from the following list.)
       (1) Power   (3) Obedience
       (2) Worship   (4) Intelligence

Answers:
1. Christ; 2. False; 3. (2); 4. (1); 5. (3).

6

Models of the Mind of Christ

Philippians 2:17-30

Paul stressed to the Philippian Christians the necessity of a submissive mind. The supreme example given was Jesus Christ. Paul was aware that some of his readers probably were saying that for them to follow Christ's high example was impossible. After all, Christ was the Son of God. He was human, but he also was divine. In contrast, they were ordinary human beings.

The whole section 2:17-30 is dominated by the idea of the submissive mind. The life of a person in whom "God is at work" (v. 13) expresses obedience to God and consideration for others. Paul introduced three Christian men as models or examples. These three men—himself, Timothy, and Epaphroditus— illustrated the mind of Christ in a practical way by their spirit, attitude, and actions. They had taken seriously Christ's example. They consecrated themselves to Christ in such a way that self was subdued in the service of other Christians. They were model Christians. Paul wanted his readers to know that the submissive mind (the mind of Christ) was not a luxury enjoyed by Christ alone, or by a chosen few. Having attitudes, actions, and thoughts like Christ was a necessity in order for each Christian to have a full life.

Paul had contemplated the possibility of his being put to death in Christ's cause (1:20); still, he had to wait for Christ's will. While he waited for his trial, he had to continue his ministry. Paul was aware that the extension of his life might be in line with God's purpose and serviceable to the church in Philippi (1:25). He expressed the mood in which they and he were to face his death if it came (2:17-18).

Meanwhile, Paul planned to send the Philippian church his best substitute—Timothy—whom they knew so well. Timothy would bring them news about Paul's trial and would represent him as only a dear friend could do. In addition, Timothy would instruct, correct, and edify the church during his stay. He also would bring back to Paul an account of conditions in the Philippian church.

However, before Timothy's journey, Paul would send Epaphroditus with the Philippian letter, without waiting for the final disposition of his case. Epaphroditus had been sick, and he knew that the Philippian Christians had heard about his illness. He was eager to see them to dispel any of their lingering anxiety over his illness.

The Mind of Christ in Paul (2:17-18)

Paul had been urging his readers to practice humility, obedience, and submission to the divine will. In verses 17-18, he pointed to himself as an example of what a change the mind of Christ could make in a person. No doubt, his readers knew of Paul's life before he became a Christian. Paul probably had told the Philippian Christians how he had persecuted the church. He reminded them in 3:6.

As a young man, Paul thought the Christian movement should be stopped. His passion to destroy the movement grew as his hatred for the Christians grew. He believed that their preaching spread untruths which greatly disturbed the people; therefore, his fury knew no end. He extended the persecution from Jerusalem to Damascus. But he was not the Sanhedrin's tool; he was their mover!

However, a miracle happened on the Damascus road! Paul was turned around. He gave his life to Christ through faith! When God gave him the mind of Christ—a mind of love, helpfulness, obedience, and submission—Paul's mind of prejudice, hatred, violence, and rejection changed radically.

In Rome, Paul was face-to-face with death, but the mind of Christ rendered him so selfless that he faced "the sacrificial offering" (v. 17) with joy. However, his sufferings did not begin in the Roman prison. Many years before his imprisonment, Paul compared his suffering to some rival apostles by giving an extensive list of hardships (2 Cor. 11:23-28).

Most people associate sorrow with suffering and death, but the mind of Christ enabled Paul to see suffering and death as doorways to a deeper joy in Christ. In verse 17, Paul used some terms drawn from the vocabulary of sacrifice and priesthood. The mention of his labors on behalf of the Philippian Christians seemed to suggest to him the sufferings which he would endure on their behalf. A possibility, if not a probability, existed that his life would be demanded for his labors on their behalf. Yet, Paul indicated, if that should occur he would have no regret; it would be a source of joy to him. He had done much for them, but he was willing to do more for them than he ever had done before. If necessary, he was willing to give his life for their sakes. J. B. Pidge commented on Paul's statement:

> This martyrdom he conceives of under the figure of a priest slain while he is offering sacrifice. The victim upon the altar is the faith of the Philippians, which Paul, the ministering priest, is engaged in offering up to God when he is slain and his blood is poured out—a most holy and precious libation.[1]

The "libation" (v. 17) was a drink offering poured out on the ground to honor a deity. Paul again was referring to the prospect of his being put to death; he thought of his life's blood as a libation poured out to God. If he must die, he would offer his life to God as a tribute of gratitude and love in behalf of his beloved Philippian friends. He was ready for service or sacrifice.

Paul did not consider his life too dear a sacrifice to be made on behalf of the Philippian Christians. He called on them to rejoice with him that such a great honor should be his (v. 18). The prospect of death was not a cause for grief, but for joy. Paul felt no dismay, and he did not want his readers to be dismayed. The Philippian Christians were making their sacrifice with joy, and Paul rejoiced with them. They should be able to rejoice with him in the prospect of his possible martyrdom.

The mind of Christ produced a deep affection in Paul for the Philippian Christians and an intense interest in their spiritual well-being. It gave him a readiness to forget his interests and to seek their interests. It enabled him to glory, not in his success or popularity, but in his converts' faith, love, and obedience. Paul urged his readers to have the mind of Christ which was his.

The Mind of Christ in Timothy (2:19-24)

In 2:19-24, Paul continued to discuss the submissive mind. The idea of consideration for others as the outcome of the mind of Christ dominates the passage. The life God inspires (2:13) is a life that is sensitive and responsive to others.

Paul would keep Timothy in Rome for a short time after Epaphroditus left. Paul intended to keep Timothy until he saw how his (Paul's) trial would be decided (v. 23). In case he was released, Paul meant to send Timothy at once to Philippi to carry on God's work in the church. Amid people's selfishness, Timothy was dependable. He would care for the Philippian Christians' welfare. Timothy would assist the Philippian church by his presence, encouragement, and counsel; he would comfort Paul by bringing back news of the believers' Christian growth. Timothy's mission was a fresh embodiment of the considerate Christian spirit.

Despite his exposure to death, Paul hoped to be delivered. His hope was "in the Lord Jesus" (v. 19). Even where his converts' spiritual welfare was concerned, Paul wholly submitted his hopes and desires to God's will. He based his hope on the need for his doing more work for Christ at Philippi. He looked to the

Lord Jesus for the realization of his hope.

Seemingly, Paul took for granted that Timothy's visit would cheer his Philippian friends, as well as supplement Epaphroditus' information concerning Paul. Also, Paul expected to be comforted when Timothy returned with news from Philippi. But apparently, Paul had not heard from Philippi since Epaphroditus' arrival in Rome and would not hear from his friends until Timothy returned to him.

Timothy not only was to be sent to the Philippian Christians, but he was to be sent for them, on their behalf. He was to help create a happier situation in Philippi. He was to help the believers overcome their grumbling, disputing, disunity, and open tension. His reassuring and comforting tidings concerning the church and the gospel's progress among the Philippians would gladden and encourage Paul.

Sending the Best
A person might think that Paul would have been occupied wholly with his interests in the prison and that he would have been oblivious to others' interests. However, he felt a vital and deep interest in the Philippian Christians' welfare. He hoped to send to them the best man he could find to promote their spiritual development (v. 19).

Timothy was the one trusted, congenial friend and helper within Paul's reach at the time Paul wrote. As a prisoner with many needs and cares, to have a companion such as Timothy beside him was a great comfort and help to Paul. Yet Paul's needs and feelings were surrendered for the well-being of the Philippian Christians. As soon as he could determine his trial's verdict, he planned to send Timothy on an errand to Philippi. Paul saw the Philippian Christians as worthy of the best he had to give. He said that he had no one like Timothy (v. 20). Timothy was in a class by himself.

Timothy's special qualification for the mission to Philippi was that he had a genuine concern for the Philippian Christians. He had a true pastoral heart. His interest in the Philippian Christians was not forced or pretended but spontaneous and natural. The qualities which Paul had in mind were not Timothy's general gifts. They centered in his capacity to be concerned for others' well-being.

Paul knew that Timothy's concern for the church would lead him to take whatever measures were necessary to restore harmony. He was not sending Timothy on a fact-finding mission. Timothy was a responsible, trusted messenger who would strengthen Paul's appeals in his Philippian letter. He would encourage, guide, and help the Philippian Christians. Since Paul could not come, Timothy would supply the spiritual blessings which Paul would have given them if he had been able to go to Philippi. Then on his return, Timothy would be able to inform Paul more accurately about the church.

Probably, some men in Rome were willing to go on a mission to Philippi but were unable to do so at that time. Likely, others were willing to go but were not qualified. Still others may have been qualified and free to go. However, Paul indicated that he could not find anyone else like Timothy (v. 20). Timothy's uniqueness for this mission was: He had the mind of Christ.

The submissive mind does not appear suddenly, automatically in the believer's life. Timothy had to develop and cultivate the mind of Christ. As Timothy walked with the Lord and worked with Paul, he grew and developed.

The Interests of Christ

Verse 21 is a severe censure on the Christian messengers in Rome. However, Paul's words do not mean that he had no genuine Christian friends and helpers with him. Furthermore, the words do not mean that his well-known associates, such as Luke, Mark, Aristarchus, Epaphroditus, and Justus were included in the indictment. In 4:21, Paul wrote: "The brethren who are with me greet you."

"They all" (v. 21) must be interpreted with reservation. Paul was speaking of men whom he might have charged with the mission on which he was sending Timothy. Perhaps he already had asked some qualified persons to go to Philippi and had met with one refusal after another. In 1:15,17, Paul had written that not every preacher in Rome was inspired by the highest motives. He now charged them with being so engrossed in themselves, "their own interests" (v. 21), that they had no time for the important work of the Lord.

Paul expected a great deal of Christian leaders. Some leaders in Rome well may have felt that he expected too much. He had asked some of them to drop their interests for months and make the long journey to Philippi. When he proposed that they should visit Philippi, they declined by making various excuses. Of those willing to go, Timothy alone qualified. He was not interested in promoting any party or in supporting any divisive cause. He was interested only in the spiritual welfare of God's people, a natural concern for him.

The interests "of Jesus Christ" (v. 21) were those interests Paul laid on the Christian leaders. The inference from this statement is that those who help Christ's people help Christ. Paul learned the opposite of this truth on the Damascus road: He learned that the one who persecutes Christ's people persecutes Christ. Paul (Saul) persecuted the Christians, but the voice of the living Lord said, " 'Saul, Saul, why do you persecute me?' " (Acts 9:4). Paul learned that Christ is identified so closely with his people that whatever one does or does not do to his people he does or does not do to Christ.

Timothy's Credentials

Timothy, a well-tried and faithful servant of the Lord, had proved himself qualified and trustworthy (v. 22). He had stood the tests, and his virtue had been proved. As Paul's spiritual son (1 Cor. 4:17), he had served Paul with devotion. At the same time, he had served with Paul as a fellow servant of Jesus Christ in expanding the gospel.

Paul's readers were able to substantiate his opinion of Timothy, for they knew Timothy's approved character. Twice, Timothy had been in Philippi with Paul (Acts 16:1,3; 19:22; 20:3-6). He may have been there at other times, for Paul repeatedly sent him on special missions to the churches (1 Cor. 4:17; 16:10).

The original construction of verse 22 is broken in the middle. Probably, Paul began as if to write, As a son serves a father Timothy has served me. But Paul's sense of propriety restrained him from writing of anyone serving him, so he wrote, "He has served with me." Paul raised Timothy to the position of an equal, a fellow laborer. This united service was for the progress of the gospel.

The Philippian Christians would not feel that Paul was sending them some mediocre substitute. As Paul's son in the faith, Timothy had proved himself faithful. He had an unselfish spirit that made him useful in the Lord's service and dependable on Paul's errands. The young protégé was happy to let Paul use him to the fullest extent. Timothy had the mind of Christ. Others were concerned with their interests, but Timothy's one desire was to serve Christ and to serve Paul.

Paul's Hope

After discussing Timothy's virtues in verses 20-22, Paul resumed his thought expressed in verse 19: sending Timothy to Philippi. Paul expected to send Timothy as soon as he learned the issue of his trial (v. 23). That issue still was uncertain. However, that Paul was looking for some immediate change in his condition is evident. Whether acquittal or execution awaited him, Paul could not tell. However, he promised that as soon as the verdict had been given, faithful Timothy would inform the Philippian Christians.

Paul did not know the outcome of his trial, but he waited in an attitude of hope and "trust" (v. 24). He did not long to die in order to escape from the troubles and burdens of his life. With confidence in Christ and with a recognition of his ministry's importance, he hoped that he could send news of his release. In addition, he trusted the Lord to enable him to visit the Philippian Christians.

Paul's mind fluctuated between the prospects of death and of being set free. From moment to moment, his outlook seemed to change. But he never expressed the slightest hint of worry or fear. The peace of Christ reigned in his heart.

"In the Lord" indicates the consciousness of a life so absorbed in Christ that it cannot think or live except in the mind of Christ. Paul's whole life was centered in Christ. (See Gal. 2:20.)

The Mind of Christ in Epaphroditus (2:25-30)

Epaphroditus was the third model of the humble and self-sacrificing service which Paul urged the Philippian Christians to imitate. Epaphroditus, a Christian who thought like Paul and Timothy, is mentioned only in this letter. He was from the Philippian church. The name Epaphras is the contracted form of Epaphroditus, but the name was a common one; no reason exists to identify Epaphroditus with the church in Colossae (Col. 1:7-8; 4:12; Philem. 23).

The Philippian church sent Epaphroditus with supplies for Paul's needs. On his arrival in Rome, he proved to be of invaluable help to Paul. However, he became ill and nearly died. News of his illness, but not his recovery, reached Philippi. Somehow, the news of his Philippian friends' great concern about his illness reached Rome.

Epaphroditus' illness and the Philippian Christians' anxiety for him concerned Paul. When Epaphroditus became homesick, Paul immediately sent him to Philippi. He probably sent this letter by him.

A Valued and Valuable Servant

Timothy would be coming to Philippi soon; Paul expected to follow, but his trip was uncertain. At the least, he might be delayed. Paul decided that his Philippian friends should be relieved of their anxiety. They needed encouragement and admonition. Paul regarded it as "necessary" to send Epaphroditus back to Philippi (v. 25). The Greek word translated "necessary" means indispensable.

Paul described Epaphroditus in relation to himself as a "brother," "fellow worker," and "fellow soldier" (v. 25). These words evidently are arranged in an ascending order.

The word "brother" was a term adopted by the early Christians to express their fraternal love for each other in Christ. This use of the word probably went back to Jesus. In the disintegrating world of the first century, Jesus drew to himself people from all divisions of humanity and said to them, "You have one teacher, and you are all brethren" (Matt. 23:8). He placed the love of neighbor with the love of God as his followers' supreme obligation.

Jesus' disciples were brothers because they had one Father, God. The fatherhood which made them brothers was that which

Saymora

5. Paul's exhortation concerning Libertinism (3:17-24)

1. Example of Christians (v.17)

2. Enemies of the Cross (vv 18-19)

3. Encouragement of Christ (3:20 - 4:1)

Paul's concluding Exhortations (4:2-9)

1. Live in Harmony (vv 2-5)

1. Work out your Problem (v-2)

2. Help others work out Problem (v3)

3. Be a good Example (vs 4-5)

2. Pray! (vs. 6-7)

(1). Perplexity. forbidden (6 A)

(2). Prayer Enjoined √6 B

(B) Peace promised v-7

3 Be Excellent! W (8-9)

(1) Think Excellent things √8

(2) Do Excellent things √9

Paul's thank you not 4 (10-20)

(1) Receiving the circumstance
√vs 10-13

(2) Opportunity to Minister
√c

(3) Adaptity to D circumst
√11-12)

(4) Confidence = Christ √13

True, honest, just, pure,
lovely: good report,
Virtue & weary praise) —

2 Rejoicing - in His gift (v. 13)
1) Righteousness of the gift
(14 - 16)

2) Reason for the gift (17)

3) Reception of the gift (18)

3) Reminding with his prayer
vv 19-20

1). God is able (19)

2. God is pround (20)

Paul's Epistany Conclusion
4:21-23
1 Final Instructo - 21a
2. Final greeting vv 21b-22)
3 Final Benedc (v 23)

imparted the new life of sonship through Christ.

When Paul called Epaphroditus "brother," he used a title that predominates in the later New Testament writings. The early Christians' adoption of the title expressed the church's unity. The mind of Christ in believers overcame the Roman world's divisive and disintegrating forces. This ideal of brotherhood in the church was the closest of all human relationships and the only one that implied equality.

Paul also wrote that Epaphroditus was his "fellow worker" (v. 25). That Epaphroditus labored with Paul in Philippi is possible. That he assisted Paul in Rome and may have become ill as a result of his work there also is possible (2:30). The word indicates that Epaphroditus was engaged in the same work that Paul was doing.

In addition, Paul wrote that Epaphroditus was his "fellow soldier" (v. 25). This term emphasizes the struggle of daring and suffering which warfare implies. Some aspects of the soldiers' business make it strange that it should be chosen to illustrate the work of Christ's ministers. But many qualities are brought out in warfare which can be used in Christ's service. The outstanding quality of military discipline is unhesitating, unquestioning obedience. Epaphroditus and Paul gave that kind of obedience to Christ.

In relation to the Philippian Christians, Paul said that Epaphroditus was their "messenger and minister to my need" (v. 25). The Greek word translated "messenger" literally is apostle. Epaphroditus was the Philippian Christians' apostle sent on an errand. He had brought the Philippian church's gifts to Paul. The Greek word translated "minister" was used to refer specifically to temple service. Paul implied that the things Epaphroditus had done for him were of a religious nature because they also were done for the Lord.

Reasons for Epaphroditus' Return

In verse 26, Paul gave two reasons why it was necessary to send Epaphroditus back to Philippi. First, Epaphroditus was so homesick that he fervently longed for the saints in Philippi (v. 26). The Greek indicates that he had a persistent case of homesickness. Second, he was distressed because of the effect which the news of his illness had had on his friends in the Philippian church. The Greek word translated "distressed" (v. 26) implies heartsickness—restless, unsatisfied weariness—

produced by some overwhelming distress.

Paul assured the Philippian Christians that the report of Epaphroditus' illness was true, for "indeed he was ill" (v. 27). His illness almost had been fatal, but God had restored him. God had showed mercy, not only on Epaphroditus, but also on Paul. Paul confessed that if Epaphroditus had died, Paul would have had "sorrow upon sorrow" (v. 27), for Epaphroditus' death would have been grief added to that caused by Paul's imprisonment.

In verse 28, Paul added two more reasons why sending Epaphroditus to Philippi was necessary. First, Paul wanted the Philippian Christians to rejoice on seeing Epaphroditus fully recovered and with them again. Second, the Philippians' joy would make Paul's burden lighter.

Paul was eager to express his thanks for the Philippian Christians' gifts and also to send news to them. However, Epaphroditus' illness increased that desire, and Paul decided to send Epaphroditus before he normally would have.

Epaphroditus' recovery and safe return would prevent Paul's experiencing "sorrow upon sorrow" (v. 27); the sorrow of imprisonment, enforced inactivity, and concern for the furtherance of the gospel would remain. But he would be less sorrowful because he thought of the joyful greeting in Philippi between Epaphroditus and the Christians.

A Man Worthy of Honor

Paul may have wanted to ward off others' criticism of Epaphroditus for leaving Paul before his release from prison. Therefore, Paul stated that he had decided to send Epaphroditus to Philippi to relieve the Philippian Christians' anxiety over Epaphroditus' health. Paul also wanted a cordial reception for Epaphroditus. That the internal factions among the Philippian believers had made Epaphroditus unacceptable to some is possible. Therefore, Paul stated the manner in which the church should receive Epaphroditus. Epaphroditus deserved more than a joyful welcome. Paul added, "Honor such men" (v. 29). He meant that those who had proved themselves willing to surrender their lives to Christ should be shown respect.

Paul concluded his discussion by telling the Philippian Christians why honor should be accorded Epaphroditus (v. 30). His service to Christ had caused Epaphroditus to expose himself to the peril of losing his life. Probably, the phrase "risking his life" refers to more than Epaphroditus' illness. Likely, it also refers to the dangers he encountered in Rome as an intimate and constant attendant of a prisoner who might be executed.

The Greek word translated "risking" was a gambler's word. It means to risk everything on a turn of the dice. Epaphroditus had staked his life as a gambler stakes his money. He had carried out Christ's work with all that it demanded in the way of sacrifice and service. He did so by completing the service of the Philippian church to Paul.

Paul did not imply that the Philippian Christians lacked anything in their service to him or that Epaphroditus had done what they had failed to do. Paul paid courteous tribute to both the Philippian believers and to Epaphroditus. He said that the gift had come from the whole church. All that was lacking to make it complete was his Philippian friends' presence. As their presence was not possible, Epaphroditus had sought to supply the lack of their presence in the service rendered to Paul. Epaphroditus did that which their absence prevented them from doing. His health broke down in his efforts to make up for the absence of other Philippian Christians. In this case, the "work of Christ" (v. 30) consisted in ministering to Paul's needs.

Lessons for Life from the Scriptures

Imitation is a principle of human life. Imitation is the means by which a great part of knowledge and a large number of habits are acquired from generation to generation. It is powerful in molding character and in controlling and directing life. Jesus was the supreme example and model for Christians. He was the God-Man, and in him the mind of God was revealed. This mind of God led him into a self-forgetting ministry of love. In order to do God's will, he placed the interests of self behind and below those of others. By precept and example, he taught his followers that true greatness forgets self, covets nothing that it cannot communicate, and dies in the hope of being raised up.

Jesus was an example or a model, but he was more. By obedience to God's will, he won over self-interest in his life. He can repeat that triumph in the life of anyone in whom he now lives. The nails that fastened him to the cross set him free to enter the life of every person who is responsive to him. Paul, Timothy, and Epaphroditus are evidences that we can win victory over egotism, pride, self-interest, and self-worship. These servants of

Christ were concerned about others. They served Christ by serving people. We, too, serve Christ by ministering to others.

Every Christian's aim should be to live in Christ. Divisive quarreling is not in harmony with the mind of Christ. The fellowship of Christians with Christians in unity is one of the greatest aids to living in Christ. Unity nurtures individual growth and lends strength and support to Christians in their sometimes difficult pilgrimages as persons.

----

1. J. B. Gough Pidge, "Commentary on the Epistle to the Philippians," *An American Commentary on the New Testament,* ed. Alvah Hovey, Vol. V (Philiadelphia: The American Baptist Publication Society, 1896), p. 35.

Personal Learning Activities

1. In Philippians 2:17-30, Paul used three Christians as models of minds submissive to Christ. From the following list, select the correct three names.

   _____ (1) Paul   _____ (4) Demas

   _____ (2) Silas   _____ (5) Tychicus

   _____ (3) Timothy   _____ (6) Epaphroditus

2. Paul was reluctant to give his life as a sacrifice on behalf of the Philippian Christians. True _____ False _____

3. If Paul were released from prison, he intended to send _____ to carry on the work in Philippi.

4. Paul indicated that he would send the Philippian letter by _____ , who had been ill.

5. With three striking designations, Paul described the Philippian Christians' messenger sent to minister to him. From the following list, select the correct responses.

   _____ (1) Fellow slave   _____ (4) Fellow worker

   _____ (2) Brother   _____ (5) Fellow soldier

   _____ (3) Friend   _____ (6) Saint

Answers:
1. (1), (3), (6). 2. False. 3. Timothy. 4. Epaphroditus. 5. (2), (4), (5).

7

Warning Against False Teachers

Philippians 3:1-11

In the first two chapters of Philippians, Paul had been concerned with the internal dissensions, mild though they were, that endangered the harmony and unity of the Philippian church. In 3:1-11, he turned his attention to a danger that was threatening the church from without: false teachers.

The false teachers may have been Pharisaic Jews who were seeking to win the Gentile converts to Christianity over to Judaism (3:2,4-6). One would think that in their proud isolation and exclusivism, the Pharisaic Jews would not have been interested in evangelizing converts from paganism. However, Josephus (the Jewish historian of the first century) told of the Pharisees' zealous propagation of the Jewish religion; in some cases, they forced circumcision on conquered peoples. They resorted to all kinds of persuasion. And they rejoiced in triumph when they enrolled a heathen convert as a member of their party, especially if the heathen was wealthy or of the noble class.

But the Pharisees' zeal was party zeal. Party spirit had taken the place of God in their lives; they worked hard for their party. Their converts became more bigoted, more devoted to party, narrower and more exclusive, and prouder of the privilege of Judaism than even those who had been born Jews. Pupils in error and vice often surpass their teachers. The false teachers in Philippi may have been Pharisees seeking to proselyte the Christian Gentiles.

Since Paul's conversion on the Damascus road (Acts 9:23), the Jews, especially the Pharisees, had opposed him and his gospel of grace through faith for all people. Their spiritual pride and exclusive bigotry continually were roused by his message. They could not endure the notion of others' being admitted freely to the same religious privileges with them. This always had been the sin of the Jews. They failed to realize their position in the world as the prophetic nation for the good of the whole earth. Instead, they indulged the self-exalting opinion that God's highest blessings were only for them. Earlier, in Pisidian Antioch, the Jews listened to Paul's preaching with great interest when he told them of the promised Messiah. However, on the following sabbath they had been filled with indignation when they learned that the Messiah was "a light for the Gentiles" as well as for them (Acts 13:16-51). The false teachers at Philippi may have been Jews who felt that Paul was perverting Judaism with his preaching. Their object was to turn the newly converted Gentile Christians into Jewish proselytes who would differ from other Jews in their recognition of Jesus as the Messiah.

The false teachers in Philippi may have been Judaizers (3:17-19). Judaizers were Jewish Christians who insisted on retaining the rites and ceremonies of the Jewish law and observing Jewish customs. They sought to combine the gospel of Christ with the observation of Jewish ceremonies. They claimed that the Law was of permanent validity and prescribed these Jewish practices. No one could be a member of God's people without observing the rites, ceremonies, and customs.

The Judaizers held that circumcision was indispensable for full status as Christians. Circumcision naturally would lead to the adoption of all the Jewish observances, which the Gentile converts constantly would hear in the Jewish services.

The Judaizers probably expected that a majority of Jews would accept Jesus as the Messiah and that the church would be more successful in evangelizing Jews than Gentiles. Therefore, they imagined that if uncircumcised Gentiles were admitted into full membership in the church, this policy would repel prospective converts from Judaism. This belief might have soothed their consciences as Christians as they pressed their doctrine and opposed Paul.

From the outset of Paul's missionary career, the Judaizers had been his chief opponents. They were bigots, but they seemed to have been honest in their belief that the historic faith of Abraham, Isaac, Jacob, and Moses was at stake. In Galatians and Colossians, Paul refuted their claims.

Spiritual Joy (3:1)

Possibly, at this point Paul contemplated ending the epistle. He frequently used the word "finally" to introduce a practical conclusion after the doctrinal part of his letters. However, the word translated "finally" (3:1) may not be used to indicate a conclusion but to indicate a transition to another important phase of Christian experience. The Greek word translated "finally" also was used with the meaning of henceforth or for the future (Acts 27:20; 7:29; 2 Tim. 4:8). Paul intimated that in addition to what he already had written, he had an exhortation to add. He summed up his teaching to this point in the epistle with a command: "Finally [or for the future], my brethren, rejoice in the Lord" (Phil. 3:1).

The keynote of Philippians is joy. Sixteen allusions to joy occur in it. Joy is the believer's appropriate response to the "good news of a great joy" (Luke 2:10) which constitutes the gospel. Joy was exemplified in Jesus' life and teachings. In the dark days of disappointment that followed the crucifixion, the disciples' joy passed under a cloud. But after the resurrection—still more on the day of Pentecost—it emerged more gloriously than before. It remained a characteristic of the early church (Acts 2:46). Joy is one of the fruits of the Spirit (Gal. 5:22), and "joy in the Holy Spirit" is an essential mark of the kingdom of God (Rom. 14:17). In Christ, Christians rejoiced "with unutterable and exalted joy" (1 Pet. 1:8) in spite of their temporary afflictions. Christian joy is no mere gaiety that knows no gloom; it is the result of faith's triumph over adverse and trying circumstances.

The warning in the second part of verse 1 is introduced with the admission that it had been given many times before. Paul declared that he did not hesitate to repeat himself because he knew that the warning concerned his friends' safety.

"The same things" (v. 1) may refer to Paul's former warnings to the Philippian saints against the dangerous teachers who would lead them astray. Paul undoubtedly had mentioned this problem to the church in Philippi, because it was present in most of the early Christian churches. However, "the same things" may refer to the Philippian letter's constant admonition to "rejoice in the Lord." To repeat this admonition was not grievous to Paul, but safe for the Philippian believers. Christian joy has a close connection with safety, because joy implies faith; more than that, it implies Christ's presence.

The phrase "to write the same things" (v. 1) may refer to what Paul had written in a previous letter to the Philippian Christians, or to what he had written in this epistle. If he was referring to what he had written in this letter, the phrase could allude to the duty of rejoicing or to the duty of maintaining unity in the church.

Warning Against False Teachers (3:2-3)

Strong Denunciation

Paul's intense feelings pierce one's thoughts as three times he repeated, "Look out" (v. 2). This repetition expressed an urgent insistence. However, Paul was not indulging in mere retorts when he called the false teachers "dogs," "evil-workers," and "those who mutilate the flesh." This threefold description referred to one kind of false teacher, not three different types, whether Jews or Judaizing Christians. The article "the" must be retained before each description.

Nearly all people have their conventions about using animal names as insults. As Jesus called Herod Antipas a "fox" (Luke 13:32) and referred to some people as "swine" and "dogs" (Matt. 7:6), Paul called the false teachers "dogs" (Phil. 3:2).

The word "dog" was a term of reproach among both the Jews and the Greeks. The word was representative of certain human qualities. For the Jews, the word "dog" stood for uncleanness and degradation. For the Greeks, the term stood for ferocity, imprudence, and greediness.

In the Bible, the term "dog" always is used to denote contempt, reproach, or dread (Deut. 23:18; 1 Sam. 24:14; 2 Kings 8:13; Rev. 22:15). It always stands for the lowest quality of life. Jews regarded Gentiles as dogs. The Jews considered the unclean feeding of these wild animals to be similar to the Gentile freedom in eating all kinds of meats. To call a person a dog was one of the strongest expressions of contempt (1 Sam. 17:43). (In Mark 7:27, Jesus' word for "dogs" in his conversation with the Syrophoenician woman is the diminutive form. His word was a softer term, "little dogs.")

By the use of the term "dogs," Paul no doubt meant to express strong disapproval of the false teachers' character and course of life. In the most solemn manner, he warned his readers against them.

The term "dog" was a figurative description of the false teachers' character, but the term "evil-workers" was a literal description of their activity. They probably were sure that they were workers of righteousness. In their view, the way of righteousness was to keep the Law in its countless rules and regulations. However, Paul was certain that the effect of their teaching was to take people farther away from God instead of bringing them nearer to God.

Instead of helping Christians grow in grace, the false teachers were hindering them. They were drawing the Christians' attention away from Christ to an outworn ritual. They were not set on doing evil; but they were fanatical, unbalanced, and unable to distinguish between a part and the whole.

By the use of the term "evil-workers," Paul intended to denote that the false teachers' zeal and labor were directed toward the distortion and perversion of the pure doctrine of justification by faith. Theirs was destructive work.

When God entered into his covenant relationship with Abraham, he commanded circumcision as an everlasting sign of the covenant (Gen. 17:7-14). It was to be a mark on the Hebrews that they were set apart as worshipers of God. However, the Jews had come to regard circumcision alone as setting them apart for God. They regarded the physical badge as making them God's chosen, thus making everything else unnecessary. They claimed that salvation depended on circumcision instead of circumcision's being a part of the covenant.

The false teachers in Philippi were insisting that the Christians should undergo circumcision in order to complete their salvation. In a contemptuous play on words, Paul refused to recognize that those sticklers for circumcision really had been circumcised. The Greek word translated "mutilate the flesh" (v. 2) is a parody of the word *circumcision*. A kindred word was used in the Septuagint to describe such cuttings forbidden by the Law (Lev. 21:5; Deut. 14:1).

Thus, Paul refused to admit that the false teachers who were insisting that the Christians in Philippi be circumcised had been circumcised. They had cut their bodies to no purpose; no real meaning was connected with it. They simply were cutters of their bodies, as the priests of Baal in Elijah's time had been

(1 Kings 18:28). The false teachers had no more reason for mutilating their bodies than the heathen had for lacerating their bodies in connection with their religion.

The false teachers' view of the circumcision rite had reduced it to a mutilation of the body. The rite had been substituted for faith in God and had lost its real meaning.

The True Circumcision

When Paul said, "We are the true circumcision" (v. 3), he claimed for himself and his readers the privilege of being the heirs of the age-long program of salvation. He thought of himself and his friends in Philippi as individually chosen by God to be recipients of the promises of grace. They were God's chosen people, individually born again, individually and collectively the heirs of the divine purpose of God's grace. Paul saw that the church was the new Israel.

The "true circumcision" (v. 3) is something inward and consists in the discarding of life's impurities and the heart's insensitiveness (Rom. 2:25-29; Col. 2:11). It does not consist of outward operation but of inward consecration. The Jew was set apart by circumcision as a worshiper of God; the Christian is set apart as a worshiper of God by the dynamic influence of God's Spirit in that person's life. All who have put their faith in God through Christ have undergone true circumcision (Rom. 2:28-29).

Paul stated three characteristics of the truly circumcised. First, they are the people who "worship God in Spirit" (v. 3). If "God is spirit" (John 4:24), those who worship him must by force of the divine arrangement worship him—if they worship him at all—in spirit. Worship must correspond to God's nature. People, because they are created in God's image, possess the power of honoring, praising, thanking, and loving God. Worship in spirit is worship in which the human spirit communes intimately with the divine Spirit (Eph. 6:18) as opposed to Jewish worship which predominantly was form without substance. Not that worship is to be confined to secrecy; it may—and will—find expression in song and speech. But all utterance and forms of worship derive their value and power from their being the manifestation of spiritual life.

Second, the true circumcision "glory in Christ Jesus" (v. 3). They depend totally on Christ. Their attitude toward Christ is exultant confidence. They glory only in what God has done and is doing for and in them through Christ. Christ receives all the honor, and his name alone is glorified. This is the essential distinction of Christians. (See 1 Cor. 1:31.) Those who honor Christ are in contrast to those who glory in external ceremonies and legal observances. This was the serious fault of the false teachers in Philippi.

Third, the true circumcision "put no confidence in the flesh" (v. 3). They distrust self. They place no ultimate confidence in anything apart from Christ. They place their confidence in God's grace and mercy. In present-day usage, the word "flesh" is a description of the grosser aspects of immorality. But this was not Paul's use of the word in this passage. For Paul, the word "flesh" in verse 3 described a person who had not received God's life through Christ. He used the word in verse 3, as Jesus did in John 3:3-7, to describe a person's condition from birth to the new birth. The word often was used to describe the whole self independent of God. It included all that belonged to humanity apart from God.

Paul's Ground for Confidence in the Flesh (3:4-6)

Paul had attacked the false teachers and had insisted that the Christians, not the Jews, were the truly circumcised and God's covenant people. The false teachers who were endangering the Christians' peace in Philippi would charge that he did not know what being a Jew meant. Therefore, Paul set out his credentials. He wanted the false teachers to know that he was a Jew in the highest sense of the term and that deliberately, knowingly, and willingly he had abandoned "flesh" for Christ.

The Futility of Flesh
Paul changed the pronoun from "we" to "I" (v. 4). The Philippian Christians, who were Gentiles, could not claim the external privileges which the Jews claimed. Paul could claim them to the full. If ever a Jew could hope to find favor with God, Paul was he. Just as the exhortation to self-giving was enforced by Christ's example (2:5-8), so the warning against the false teachers was enforced by Paul's experience.

Paul knew the futility of trying to attain salvation by means of the "flesh." He had renounced confidence in the flesh; but for the moment, he took up the false teachers' claim as he challenged his readers to compare the teachings. He claimed to be in a better position for confidence in the flesh than any of them.

Paul's object was to show that he did not despise the "flesh" because he did not possess it, but because it had no value in salvation. Once he had confidence in the flesh, but he saw that it could not gain salvation for him.

Inherited Privileges

Paul listed some of his prerogatives and privileges which once had filled his heart with confidence and pride. In verses 5-6, he illustrated what he meant by "flesh." The four clauses in verse 5a describe four privileges he inherited.

Paul was "circumcised on the eighth day" (v. 5). He was born of the covenant people, a true Israelite. He belonged to Israel by birth. He came from a family that was meticulous in its fulfillment of prescribed duties. He was circumcised in exact compliance with the Law. (See Gen. 17:12; Lev. 12:3.) If any ground of confidence existed from such compliance with the Law, he had it. He was a pure Jew.

Paul was "of the people of Israel" (Phil. 3:5). He was a direct descendant of Jacob, whose name *Israel* was bestowed on him by God (Gen. 32:28). The name "Israel" gave the Hebrews their cherished name *Israelites* which designated them as God's covenant people. Paul's parents neither belonged to a mixed stock nor had been grafted into Israel. He was a direct descendant of Abraham, Isaac, and Jacob. He belonged, by pure blood, to the chosen, covenant, specially privileged people.

Paul was "of the tribe of Benjamin" (v. 5). His family had preserved their genealogy. He did not belong to a renegade tribe. He descended from the tribe which gave Israel's first king, which had a foremost place among Israel's armies (Judg. 5:14), and which never gave up its allegiance to the house of David. Paul belonged to the tribe within whose boundary Jerusalem stood. He belonged to the tribe which, along with Judah, formed the nucleus of the new nation after the exile.

The tribe of Benjamin had a special place in Israel's aristocracy. Benjamin and Joseph were Jacob's favorite sons. They were born to Rachel, Jacob's favorite wife. Of Jacob's sons, Benjamin alone had been born in the Promised Land (Gen. 35:16-18). When Paul stated that he was of the tribe of Benjamin, he claimed that he belonged to Israel's aristocracy.

Paul was "a Hebrew born of Hebrews" (v. 5). This phrase was a Hebrew mode of expressing the superlative degree. With this statement, Paul claimed that he enjoyed every advantage which possibly could be derived from being a Hebrew. Although born in Tarsus, he was of pure Jewish descent; and he maintained his Jewish customs and manner of life. He was no Grecized or Hellenistic Jew. (See Acts 22:3-4.) Many Jews who were scattered over the Roman Empire practiced the Jewish religion but did not use the Hebrew language or conform to Jewish customs. These were Hellenists. Paul's parents reared him as strictly as if he had been born in Judah. His family spoke the Hebrew language and retained the Hebrew customs. Paul spoke Hebrew (Acts 21:40) and used the Hebrew Scriptures as well as the Greek translation. He was a thorough Hebrew.

Achieved Distinctions

Having enumerated his inherited privileges, Paul wrote of matters which depended on his choice. In verses 5b-6, he mentioned three religious characteristics which he had achieved.

Paul was "a Pharisee." (See Acts 22:3; 23:6; 26:5.) Today, the Pharisees have come to be regarded as the embodiment of pride and self-righteousness. However, in Paul's day they stood for the purest, strictest morality. They were the strictest sect of the Jews. They were devoted to the Law and were the nation's orthodox party. The Pharisees were Judaism's most loyal, patriotic, and religious party. They maintained the Law amid the indifference of their time. They distinguished themselves among the Jewish sects by their rigid adherence to the letter of the Law. These purists endeavored to guard the Law from any possible violation by throwing around it a vast body of traditions. To the Jews in Paul's day, the Pharisees had reached the highest summit of religious experience.

As a Pharisee, Paul had given himself wholly to know the Law, to keep it, and to teach it. He adopted the most respectful and submissive attitude possible toward the Law. His overriding concern was to live in conformity to what he believed were God's regulations for every detail of life. He was not only a Pharisee, but he probably was the son of a Pharisee. (See Acts 26:5.) He had been educated in Jerusalem in the most famous school of the Pharisees "at the feet of Gamaliel."

Paul had been "a persecutor of the church" (v. 6). He once considered the persecution of the church a virtue and a meritorious work. In defending the Jewish faith, he had done all in his power to exterminate Christians. He did not become a persecutor because he was untrue to the best traditions of his faith. He sought to destroy the church because of his ardent fidelity to his faith.

Paul had been "under the law blameless" (v. 6). From a legal standpoint—according to the letter of the Law and as other people saw him—he had been blameless. He had fulfilled every demand of the Law. He had practiced the strict Pharisaic codes exactly and without fault. He had kept all the Commandments, and his outward conduct had been irreproachable.

In outward grounds of confidence, no one else could surpass Paul. He had had all the privileges of Judaism. All that he enumerated—his stock in trade as a devotee of Judaism—merely had contributed to his self-approbation. He had had "confidence in the flesh" (v. 4). He had gloried in what he was and what he did. His ego had been pleased; others had approved and praised him; but throughout, God had not been involved.

Loss, and Immeasurable Gain (3:7-8)

All the things mentioned in verses 5-6 had advantaged Paul as a Jew. They had given him a reputation among the people, had laid the foundation of his aspirations and hopes, and, above all, had satisfied his conscience. But now those advantages were valueless in his sight. He summed up and renounced all of them. More than that, he counted them as loss.

Paul's fancied merits had kept him from receiving Christ into his life. As soon as he met Christ on the road to Damascus, the wasted years of self-righteousness pressed painfully on him. He wondered how he could have neglected such a Savior so long. He realized now that anything which shut Christ out of life inflicted a distinct loss on life.

Paul never meant that his circumcision, ancestry, energy, diligence, and law-keeping were, in themselves, evil. But he found them evil in the sense that they shut out Christ from his life. As substitutes for Christ, they were not only worthless, they were loss. Every day he relied on them had been a day of deprivation in regard to salvation. However, when Paul met Christ, the things that he had believed to be his glory were "counted as loss" (v. 7). All his "gain" was laid aside in order that he might accept God's grace through Christ. He divested himself of "flesh" (3:3, what he could do) that he might accept salvation in Christ.

Paul widened the range of loss to include "everything" (v. 8).

He not only counted outward privileges and prerogatives as loss because of Christ, but he counted all things as loss in comparison with the life of God shared with him through Christ. The emphasis is on the word "everything" (Greek, all things) which includes everything that could be imagined, that Paul still possessed, that he might attain. It included all that the "flesh" still could take hold of and turn into a ground of separate confidence and boasting.

On the Damascus road, Christ came into Paul's life. Christ became the ground, meaning, and aim of his life. His life found its explanation, worth, and loving imperative in Christ. All else that once had value to him fell away. If not entirely dismissed, they were to have such place and use only as Christ assigned to them. And all new attainments that Paul might achieve could have only a subordinate place to Christ.

Paul's opening his heart and surrendering his life to Christ had not been merely the matter of one hour of high feeling and deep impression. The experience had continued in full force. This experience was not a matter of inward feeling only. Paul had been tested and proved. He had suffered the loss of all things as the result of his unflinching faith and service. He counted all to be lost for Christ. His believing mind was a changed mind in regard to all these things.

The words "knowing Christ" (v. 8) mean much more than knowledge about Christ. Paul had this kind of historical information before he was converted. To know Christ means to have a personal relationship with him through faith. It means a close intimacy with Christ from which springs an ever-growing acquaintance of his spirit and will. To know Christ is to know God, and to know God is eternal life. (See John 17:3.) For Paul, salvation was knowing Christ in a personal way.

The word translated "refuse" (v. 8) was a common word in Greek. It was used to describe any kind of refuse: dregs, rubbish, sweepings, chaff, husks, table-leavings, dung. Thus, Paul saw things that once he had valued highly as mere rubbish to be cast out of his life as worthless. No other language could express a deeper sense of the utter worthlessness of all external advantages in the matter of salvation.

Paul's Quest as a Christian (3:9-11)

In verse 8, the words "that I may gain Christ" do not mean that

Paul did not have Christ. He already had Christ, but he wished to incorporate Christ more and more into life. He had rejected the former gain in order to obtain a greater gain. By gaining Christ, he wanted to become so united with Christ that Christ progressively became his life. Since to gain Christ in this way and still hold on to his self-righteousness was impossible, Paul gladly renounced self-righteousness.

Authentic Righteousness

Verse 9 describes true righteousness. This righteousness is produced by God's Spirit through faith in Christ. Paul's self-righteousness died at the sight of the living Christ on the road to Damascus. But instead of his self-righteousness, he found a perfect righteousness provided by Christ.

The word "found" in verse 9 suggests the outcome of a trial. Paul referred to any time when a trial or test would be made. This would include scrutiny all his life, in death, and before the judgment seat. The trial would reveal his character. He wanted his life to demonstrate that he was in Christ. He did not desire to have any righteousness that could be called his. Paul wanted others to see in his life the righteousness which the Holy Spirit produced through Paul's faith in Christ.

The phrase "in him" (v. 9) refers to the life which Christ shares with all believers. Paul frequently spoke of Christians as being in Christ. Life in Christ is not a continuance of the former life under new conditions; it is a new qualitative life which is the risen Christ's heavenly life. The old life simply is not purged of its evil aspects. Life in Christ means that a person is "a new creation" (2 Cor. 5:17).

Paul's abandoning his former gain resulted in a new and true kind of righteousness, a righteousness which included being right and doing right. Both were provided in Christ and were received through Paul's faith in him. God's righteousness was incarnated in Christ and imparted to Paul by the indwelling Christ. Paul placed this true righteousness in contrast to any goodness which he once may have possessed. Because of his union and fellowship with God through faith in Christ, he no longer had a self-righteousness which consisted in the strict fulfillment of the Law's requirements.

The leading characteristic of the word "faith" (v. 9) is to unite. Faith is not mere assent to testimony, a mental act separable from personal trust or reliance. The derived meaning of the word

stresses the idea of personal reliance. It also involves distrust in self and trust only in Christ. Believers are united with Christ by God's grace through faith.

A Continuing Process

Paul indicated (v. 9) that he had been given God's "righteousness." "Righteousness" means doing right as well as being right. Because righteousness means being and doing, Paul showed (v. 10) that he had been introduced into the strictest moral enterprise. Characteristically, Paul portrayed Christian growth as gaining Christ or becoming like Christ. If Christians are satisfied with Christ for salvation, they cannot be satisfied with themselves until they are like him.

Another aspect of gaining Christ consisted in Paul's more complete knowledge of Christ (v. 8). He repeated the thought with deeper emphasis and showed its wider meaning. His submission to Christ's will was not attained instantly when he was converted. His spiritual growth was a gradual process. The great change from sin and self-righteousness to God's righteousness was not the work of a day but the slow and patient process of a lifetime. However complete Paul's surrender, it was a continuous process, a deepening experience.

Paul desired to "know him" (Christ, v. 10). In the Bible, the word *knowledge* in regard to persons means entrance into the deepest personal intimacy. (See Gen. 4:1.) Knowledge is not simply intellectual perception of a fact; it is a personal encounter with another person. It is an acquaintance based on experience. First, by sense or emotion, a person must perceive, possess, and understand. Consequently, Paul—having been saved by Christ—wanted to "know" him. He wanted to enter into the deepest possible union with Christ.

Paul had a strong desire to know Christ and to be like him. He had an emotion that consistently held to Christ and a will that persistently was obedient to him. Paul longed for this deepening experience until it became his supreme desire. He mentioned two features of this knowledge of Christ.

First, he wanted to know "the power of his [Christ's] resurrection" (v. 10). Christ's resurrection was a glorious manifestation of divine power. The resurrection also was the crowning point of Christ's life. It showed him to be victorious over sin and death; it was the triumph in which his life and ministry on earth ended. Christ's resurrection was God's seal on his life and ministry. It

102

also was Christ's emergence into the power and blessedness of victorious life.

The power of Christ's resurrection in Christians is God's divine energy which enables them to be victorious over sin and death. The indwelling Christ gives believers the same dynamic power that he had. Christians' ability to conquer sin's daily habit, and the possibility of living in daily holiness, are derived from the power of the resurrected Christ's living in them. (See Gal. 2:20.)

Paul knew by experience the difficulty of remaining loyal to Christ so that sin's power would not revive its mastery over him. Therefore, he wanted the power that raised Christ from the dead to surge through him and overcome sin in his life. The uncertainty emphasized Paul's need for watchful and constant striving.

Second, Paul wanted to "share his [Christ's] sufferings" (v. 10). When the risen Christ had entered into Paul and made himself manifest in Paul's conduct, the inevitable result was a sharing in Christ's sufferings. This meant dying to sin, crucifying the flesh, and suffering for the sake of Christ and his purpose. Paul was in constant danger; his fellowship with Christ in suffering might terminate in his death at any moment. He constantly prayed that he might endure his trials to the end in the same spirit with which Christ had endured his suffering and death. To share in Christ's sufferings was necessary for Paul to consider himself "dead to sin and alive to God in Christ Jesus" (Rom. 6:11).

Suffering had been a part of Paul's life since his Damascus-road experience. Paul had been a persecutor, but he had learned what it meant to be persecuted. Later he had yearned to participate more fully in the sufferings which united him more intimately with Christ.

Christ's life was, at the same time, his movement toward his death. He lived as one laying down his life, not merely in one great sacrifice at the close, but from step-to-step throughout his whole ministry. He had to do so if he was to be faithful. Pain and trial were the inevitable accompaniment of the work given him. His sufferings arose out of his conflict with sin.

Paul wanted to become like Christ "in his death" (v. 10). The words "like him in his death" reveal Paul's conviction as to the only condition on which his ambition to know Christ better could be realized. They express Paul's conviction of the completion of his death to sin.

The word translated "becoming" implies a continual process. It denotes a deep, real, inner conformity. The reference is to dying daily to self and the world.

A Future Hope

Just as no resurrection of Christ was possible without his death, so Paul could not experience resurrection without his death in Christ. In verse 11, Paul probably referred to the spiritual resurrection from his dying to sin. (See Rom. 6:5.) This resurrection is a complete resurrection, a victory over every form of death. This mystical union and fellowship of the Christian with Christ must consummate finally in the glorified, bodily resurrection with and in Christ. To one with faith, this truth is not only a present possession but also a future expectation. Ultimate resurrection is a matter of certainty, but it also is an object of hope.

Possibly, Paul was referring to his final resurrection. (See 1 Cor. 15:12-28.) However, to suppose that he had any doubt as to his final resurrection is impossible. Neither could he have thought that any excellence in Christian attainments could affect his final resurrection.

The element of hope was fundamental to all of Paul's thinking. The verb "attain" (v. 11) means to arrive at the end of a journey. It presents a figure of a pilgrimage. The life of faith is the beginning of the life of glory. The presence of God's Spirit in Paul was a reality; yet, it was no more than an earnest of his inheritance. Paul humbly hoped to attain all the blessedness of "the resurrection from the dead" (v. 11), and the blessedness simply would be an intensification of an experience already begun.

Lessons for Life from the Scriptures

A divine joy in Christ is possible for believers in spite of struggles and difficulties. Christian joy is basic confidence in Christ's presence and power. We can rejoice in Christ's fellowship, in his love and grace, and in the knowledge of his dominion over our lives and his rule over our destiny. Humbly, we can ask for the joy of living. To gain that joy, we must seek to get acquainted better with Christ each day through worship by God's Spirit, in spirit and truth.

Christ calls us to break completely with the habits and attitudes of our unconverted life. We experience progressively a complete change of thought, motive, aim, and activity. Christ's love will draw us from the remnants of the old life if we will allow it to do so. We can suffer with Christ, and we also can have his resurrection power in our lives.

Redemption is the experience of a moment in time when life is opened to Christ and given to him; but redemption also is a process, the work of a lifetime. The effort to experience more of Christ, to be more responsive to him, to mold Christian character, to adopt Christ's attitude toward people and things is an ongoing, disciplined struggle. Christian growth is not automatic; our relationship with Christ must be tended carefully if we are to make progress and develop as his persons.

Personal Learning Activities

1. The false teachers of Philippians 3:2-3 may have been (choose the proper responses):
   _____ (1) Pharisaic Jews   _____ (3) Judaizers
   _____ (2) Gnostics   _____ (4) Pagans

2. The Judaizers held that _____ was indispensable for full status as Christians. (Select the correct answer from the following list.)
   (1) Sabbath observance   (4) Observance of feast days
   (2) Ceremonial hand-   (5) Circumcision
       washing   (6) Temple sacrifice
   (3) Fasting

3. The keynote of Philippians is (choose one):
   _____ (1) Faith   _____ (3) Hope
   _____ (2) Love   _____ (4) Joy

4. Paul used strong words to refer to the false teachers. From the following list, select the terms he employed.
   _____ (1) Pagans   _____ (4) Dogs
   _____ (2) Those who muti-   _____ (5) Evil workers
           late the flesh   _____ (6) Pigs
   _____ (3) Snakes

5. By true circumcision, Paul meant physical circumcision performed by Christians. True _____ False _____

Answers:
1. (1), (3); 2. (5); 3. (4); 4. (2), (4), (5); 5. False.

8

Warning Against Laxity of Life

Philippians 3:12 to 4:3

Freedom from Judaism, a religion which relied on external conformity to rules and regulations, implied no encouragement to laxity of life. In the church in Philippi, laxity of life seemed to have been present among some of the members because of at least three assumptions they made: (1) Some assumed that perfection already had been attained (3:12-16). (2) Some assumed that Christian liberty involved the abolition of all moral restraints (3:17 to 4:1). (3) Some assumed that in the common union with Christ, people could hold disagreements, petty differences, and animosities (4:2-3).

In 3:12-16, Paul wrote of himself; however, his language really was directed against some church members who were claiming that they had reached moral perfection and were living above sin. They were claiming that they had arrived at their goal and were beyond responsibility, duty, or progress. To think of themselves in this way was to be deceived. To think that they were not responsible for their sins was to corrupt their consciences and to pervert their moral sense. Willfully, they were blinding themselves to their condition.

Possibly this error of perfectionism among some of the members had arisen because of the influence of incipient Gnosticism. This false teaching was present in the Colossian church about the same time. Also, the error may have been the result of Jewish teaching. Some Jewish teachers and others held that fellowship between God and people was impossible until people became righteous. In order to be righteous, people had to receive enlightenment and attain spiritual perfection by keeping the Law. Some members in the Philippian church were denying the presence of sin in their lives. Their view of God's exalted claims was so deficient and their estimate of their character and conduct was exaggerated so much that they thought they had arrived at sinless perfection.

Paul stated that no Christian had arrived at a sinless state. He admitted the existence of sin as a fact in every Christian, but he denied that this made fellowship with God impossible. If God did not have fellowship with sinners, he would have fellowship with no human being because all are sinners. God forgives and cleanses each Christian from sin. He is perfecting what he began and is carrying out his purpose.

All Christians are aware—and the New Testament confirms—that much evil remains to be overcome in their lives. The greatest saints of the Bible confessed their sins. Paul addressed the Corinthians, among whom scandalous sins existed, not only as saints but as those sanctified in Christ Jesus (1 Cor. 1:2). He buffeted his body and kept it under control because the old sinful self constantly was asserting itself (1 Cor. 9:27).

In 3:17 to 4:1, Paul dealt with another problem in the church: antinomianism—the casting aside of all restraints, the degenerating of freedom into license. The new freedom in Christ had been interpreted perversely by some of the members as an excuse for all manner of self-indulgence. They imagined that freedom from law meant license to sin with impunity. Paul warned against legalism that would destroy the Christian's true and proper freedom. He warned just as strongly against the perverse abuse of freedom which mocked the gospel and turned its advocates into the "enemies of the cross of Christ" (v. 18). This problem probably grew out of Paul's preaching of the gospel of grace and faith. He had preached that faith is the one condition on which a person can secure the salvation offered by God. In fact, he had taught that "where sin increased, grace abounded all the more" (Rom. 5:20).

Paul's emphasis on grace and faith was being interpreted in such a way as to destroy the foundation of any ethical obligation within the Christian life. Some of the church members seem to have concluded that they could indulge in sin to the full. Why should Christians not increase their sins so that God could exercise his grace more? To assume that the more one sinned, the more opportunity he or she would be given to display God's grace seemed logical to them. Paul indicated that these members were misunderstanding completely what was involved in God's grace. Rather than regarding grace as a license to live in sin, they should see it as a calling for gratitude to God and complete devotion to his will.

In 4:2-3, Paul dealt with the problem of disunity in the Philippian church. Internal divisions had begun to show themselves, if not in the form of regularly defined parties, at least as forces that were moving in that direction. Paul knew that if the internal divisions were not checked, they soon would lead to open rupture.

This problem of disunity had been mentioned several times before in the Philippian letter, but now it was brought into full view. The disunity was expressing itself in disagreements. The quarrels were not just private arguments; they involved the heart of the Christian community.

The quarrels alarmed Paul. His appeal for agreement rested on the fact of the church's union with Christ. So entirely is the church one with her Lord that to divide the one is to divide the other. Since Christ cannot be divided, a divided church cannot be tolerated. (See 1 Cor. 1:13.) Such a church is a standing contradiction to the unity of Christ's person.

No Christian Is Perfect (3:12-16)

Paul's Not Yet

Paul wanted the Philippian Christians to understand clearly. From the preceding verses, they should not conclude that he had reached perfection in grace and faith. He had come a long way since his Damascus-road experience. However, he still had a long way to go toward his goal of spiritual and moral maturity. His conversion was a starting place, not a stopping place. He did not accept his imperfection passively.

The Greek verb translated "obtained" (v. 12) means to win a prize. Paul's conversion was a sudden and supernatural experience; he was not led gradually from Judaism to Christianity. However, at his conversion, he did not instantly win the prize of spiritual maturity. The prize demanded a lifetime of continued effort. He knew nothing of a passive life, only a life of the greatest activity. He had not reached perfection, even at a late stage in his life.

Paul had a definite reason for writing that he had not "already obtained this or am already perfect" (v. 12). He did so because he knew some members of the church in Philippi were thinking that they had obtained and already had reached perfection. They imagined that they had reached the highest level of Christian life and had no more progress to make. Paul refuted this notion, not only by repudiating any such claim for himself, but by depicting the Christian life as strenuous and unceasing progress toward a goal.

In the last part of verse 12, Paul used one of his favorite metaphors drawn from the Greek games. He wrote of his Christian life and used the analogy of a race. The race could be won only if the runner gave his attention wholly to reaching the goal. The runner could win only if he threw all his energies into the effect to reach the goal as quickly as possible.

Paul realized that his conversion had occurred because Christ had made him his own. The initative did not come from Paul but from God. The meaning seems to be that Christ began working with him at his conversion with the express purpose that he (Paul), through faith and obedience, might be Christlike at last. Paul loved because he first was loved; he sought because he was sought by Christ. For him, the Christian life was a progressive discovery of the meaning of having been "made" Christ's own. This consisted of a personal knowledge of Christ, submission to his will, trust in him, and a continuous effort to attain his moral perfection.

Paul's One Goal

In verse 13, Paul expressed a direct and loving appeal. He wanted to enforce what he had written in verse 12. When his feelings were moved deeply and he had an important statement to make, he used the word "brethren."

In contrast to some who held a self-sufficient view of themselves—who held that they had reached perfection—Paul emphasized that he had not arrived at the goal. He was no novice when he wrote the Philippian letter. He was an old man, rich in many graces; yet, he felt that he had not reached the end of his efforts. He did not contrast his estimate of himself to other people's estimate of him. He contrasted his estimate of himself with others' estimates of themselves.

After repeating in a slightly different form the first words of the preceding sentence, Paul described his earnest efforts for Christlikeness, which he had described in the closing words of verse 12. The words "obtained" and "press on" were developed into a comparison of Paul with a runner in the races.

"I do" does not appear in the Greek which the Revised Standard Version renders: "One thing I do" (v. 13). The broken sentence recaptures Paul's excitement in the prison. He had one overmastering passion, to the exclusion of all other interests: to get to the goal of maturity and to get there swiftly. To reach that goal, Paul wrote that he was doing two things.

First, Paul was forgetting the things which were behind. He simply meant that he had broken the power of the past. He could not change the past, but he could change the meaning of the past. Some things in his past could have held him back, but they became inspirations to speed him along. The events of the past did not change, but his understanding of them changed. The statement is general, applying to past blessings, achievements, and sins. He would not allow any past experience to hinder his efforts in the present or the future. Paul's past blessings were an earnest of his future. His past achievements were stepping-stones to greater accomplishments in the future. His past sins were viewed in repentance as offering hope of the final conquest of all sin.

Second, Paul was straining forward to the things which were in front. The words "straining forward" describe a runner racing hard toward the tape with his eyes on nothing but the goal, his ardent spirit outrunning his lagging feet. Paul had one object, one aim, one great purpose in life. To this singleness of purpose he owed his extraordinary attainments.

Paul's singleness of purpose was no self-generated ambition. It was not the passionate perfectionism of a naturally ambitious person. Paul had not started his life moving in the direction of Christlikeness; Christ had taken the initiative. He had begun working in Paul for a purpose, and now Paul's ambition was to grasp that purpose and make it his.

The Coveted Prize
Paul had defined his ambition as a believer. He had confessed his failure to achieve that ambition. And he had stated his determination to press on. In verse 14, he disclosed his goal. He wrote that Christians are God's athletes. When they set themselves to fulfill the ambition of reproducing the Christlike life,

they are like runners who enter a great race.

To distinguish between what is symbolized by the "goal" and the "prize" is not necessary. Both refer to the exalted destiny to which God had summoned Paul. However, if Paul had a difference in mind, his "goal" fixed the thought on the end of the race and the "prize" on the reward which followed. The prize would be granted when the goal was reached.

The "upward call of God in Christ Jesus" is a call from God to the godly life. This call is heavenly in origin, operation, and final issue. It denotes the internal and effectual drawing of the life toward God by God's grace.

The prize was not Paul's vocation as an apostle, but the high calling which he shared with all Christians. It was the prize of Christlikeness. The goal of the Christian's life, therefore, is nothing less than Christ himself.

Christ provided the moral image toward which Paul moved and the moral power by which he could attain it. The call existed before the race began. It is the invitation, the sanction, the authority by which the race is begun and by which the prize is awarded. The "upward call" comes from and leads to the highest sphere to which a person can attain. It is a Christian's highest ideal, and the believer cannot attain anything beyond it. And this highest Christian possibility is treasured up "in Christ Jesus" (v. 14).

Real Maturity

Paul hardly would have addressed the Philippian Christians as mature when he had written that he had not attained that state (v. 12). He may have used the word "mature" or perfect in verse 15 with a touch of irony in reference to some who thought they had arrived at perfection. However, he included himself with the group; and he used the same word that was used to describe the maturity of Christians in this life.

Paul exhorted the "mature" to "be thus minded" (v. 15). Evidently he referred to his previous statements in which he had described his attitude and feelings about his Christian race. He set his example before the Philippian Christians as their pattern. He invited them to share his attitudes and feelings in order to come to a similar estimate of themselves, to imitate his effort after Christian growth. He seemed to suggest that in the Christian vocabulary, perfect or "mature" can mean only that a Christian is conscious of not being perfect or mature but has a desire to reach that goal.

Paul was writing to his dear friends in the Philippian church whom he honored with rare commendations for their fidelity and spiritual achievements. He desired all the members who knew the real nature and demands of the Christian life to agree with him about their Christian immaturity. And he wanted them to imitate his efforts toward maturity. Nevertheless, he admitted that some of the members might not agree with him about the program of Christian maturity. He did not attempt to force his conviction on them. He was far more mature than the Christians in Philippi; however, he treated their right to disagree with him with courtesy. He respected their right to think for themselves, and he was willing to wait until God opened their minds to the truth as he expounded it.

Paul indicated that if his readers would admit their immaturity and affirm their striving in Christ to become mature, God would reveal to them their defective views. God would give them more light if they would walk by the light he already had given.

Advancing Together

In verse 15, Paul stated a great principle: If the main direction of Christians' lives is right, God will reveal the points at which they are immature or wrong. However, Paul recognized that this principle easily could lead to a tolerance of evil in a person's life and also hinder efforts toward maturity. Therefore, in verse 16, he stated that the principle was true only on certain conditions. He indicated that God would reveal to Christians their wrong if—and only if—they steadfastly continued in the course which they knew to be right.

Paul seems to have emphasized two things. First, he stressed that the Philippian Christians were to keep on the same course. If they were to make progress, they would need to live up to their best knowledge of the Christian life's ideals and requirements. While they waited for fuller revelations from God, they were to make their present attainments the rule of their conduct. Believers were to walk in the truth they had received. They were to live by the highest truths that they had been able to grasp, and they were not to fall back from the point which they had attained. The Philippian Christians were not to cease their striving to advance.

Second, Paul's readers were to keep on the Christian path together; they were to move forward in the same line. Their maturity merely amounted to relative stages of imperfection; therefore, they needed to realize that all were striving for the same goal. They were to be ready to help one another rather than to criticize or envy one another. Despite all the differences of opinion which they had, the Philippian Christians were to make progress together toward the fulfillment of revealed truth.

No Christian Has License to Sin (3:17 to 4:1)

A Christian Model

Deeply moved by what he was about to write, Paul addressed the Philippian Christians with the endearing word "brethren" (v. 17). Should not brothers show that they belong to the same family?

Once more, Paul appealed to his experience. This time, he contrasted his Christian living with some members who confused liberty with license. He was aware that from all he had written, his readers knew he did not regard himself as faultless. However, they knew his manner of life and that of his fellow missionaries. Had their conduct ever encouraged moral laxity? The missionaries, collectively, had set the pattern. They had started a tradition which by its variety in detail showed that moral living was the norm for all Christians.

Paul knew the power of example, both for teaching and encouragement. So, he would not allow even humility to prevent him from bringing his example to bear on the problem in the church in Philippi. He saw that at some points, for them to imitate him was desirable (v. 17). He was concerned so greatly for their welfare that he was willing to lay himself open to the charge of conceit. The self-forgetful person will dare to do things from which the self-conscious person shrinks in modesty; yet, the former is the humbler of the two. What Paul desired the Philippian Christians to imitate were his rejection of self-sufficiency and his willingness to sacrifice all things to win Christ. He wanted them to imitate his clear sense of his imperfections, his moral life, and his eager straining toward maturity. Paul did not think of himself as the only example; he also thought of others, such as Timothy (2:19-24) and Epaphroditus (2:25-30). He did not set up as examples those who had confused Christian liberty with license. Paul urged the Philippian Christians to follow the example of those who were safe guides for Christian conduct.

Paul's appeal in verse 17 did not imply egotism or self-confidence but absolute confidence in his message and its principles. It also implied Paul's consciousness that his life, by God's grace, was molded on these principles. He did not claim to be a perfect example. He insisted that the Christian's inward aspirations must find expression in conduct that is wholly consistent with inner ideals. The pattern is Christ (Phil. 2:5-8); however, as Paul imitated Christ, he did not hesitate to give himself as an example for the Philippian Christians to follow.

Enemies of the Cross
The charge to imitate Paul and the other missionaries needed explanation. In verse 18, Paul gave the reason why he so strongly enjoined them to do so. "Many" who professed to be Christians claimed that they were free from the restraint of moral law; therefore, they lived immoral lives.

The moral laxness about which Paul wrote may have had several causes. Some church members may have taken the view, prominent in later Gnosticism, that matter essentially was evil and that the body was no better or worse because of moral conduct. Perhaps some were sheltering themselves under Paul's preaching of liberty, his assertion that the Christian is not under Law but under grace. These members were misinterpreting Paul, saying that since believers were accepted in Christ, God was indifferent to their actions. Those who viewed grace as freedom from moral restraint were called libertines or antinomians.

Against the people who were degenerating freedom into license, Paul gave a solemn warning. His tears (v. 18) were evidence that they were members of the churches. To know of people who professed Christ as their Lord and Savior and then denied him with their lives broke his heart. He declared that many made such denials and that he frequently had been compelled to warn the Philippian Christians against their influence. He repeated this warning with deep emotion.

The antinomians were enemies of the Christian life's central principle. (See Rom. 16:17-18.) *They were enemies of the cross of Christ* (v. 18). They deluded themselves in the belief that the purpose of the cross was to give free rein to sin; thus, they disgraced it in the eyes of unbelieving observers.

When Christ's cross is understood rightly and accepted, it becomes a creative principle, the power of a new view and a new course of life. To Paul, Christ's cross was not the wooden beams on which Jesus' body was fastened. It was a revelation of the measure of people's rebellion against God and God's love for people. At the cross, people did their worst against God while God did his best on behalf of people.

When a person is saved, that person is brought into a new life, which is the way of the cross. The individual is delivered from the way of self-love, self-assertion, self-worship, self-trust to the way of the cross. The way of the cross is the way of self-denial and self-giving rooted in faith in God. Paul knew of only one salvation; that salvation is accomplished in persons as God in Christ gains entrance into them and transforms them from within. According to Paul, the cross of Christ must become a living reality within people's lives. For him, the cross was a symbol of death to self and sin.

In verse 19, the enemies of Christ's cross are described more fully in a fourfold way. First, "their end is destruction." The Greek word *apōleia* translated "destruction" also means waste, ruin, perdition.

How Paul used *apōleia* in this verse is not clear. Did he mean that the antinomians were Christians and that their actions would ruin or waste their lives and testimony? Did he mean that the quality of their existence already was one of ruin? Or did he mean that these members were not Christians and would end up in eternal perdition? The Greek word will permit any of the three interpretations. Probably Paul had the first usage in mind in verse 19.

Second, "their god is the belly"; that is, the place belonging to God had been usurped by the lowest part of the antinomians' nature. Their aim was to gratify the flesh; appetite was their master. Their minds and hearts were the slaves of their appetites. Eating, drinking, and gratifying fleshly lusts had become the sum total of their lives. They had consecrated their thoughts and their energies to these things. The self-indulgence which wounded others' tender consciences and turned liberty into license was condemned.

Third, "they glory in their shame" (v. 19). That is, the antinomians' pride was in that which should have caused them shame. They not only practiced evil, but they even boasted about it. They boasted of their liberty and perverted it into license. In the name of liberty, these members were proud of what ought to have caused shame. They discarded moral restraints and paraded their evil deeds.

Fourth, the antinomians had their "minds set on earthly things." That is, their thoughts, feelings, and interests were concentrated on the material, the temporal. They allowed their concerns to be bounded by the horizon of earthly things. They had no high, heavenly thoughts and aspirations but concentrated their energies on the things of time and sense. Their minding "earthly things" was not wrong. Their error was in making "earthly things" their only concern.

Dual Citizenship

In verse 20, Paul drew a striking contrast. The "enemies of the cross of Christ" (v. 18) had set their minds "on earthly things" (v. 19). Paul and the other true Christians had the object of their attachment in heaven (v. 20). The earth was not their fatherland; heaven was the state or kingdom to which they belonged and where they enjoyed rights and privileges. Therefore, their conduct would be in agreement, not with the earthly minded, but with the heavenly minded. The word "our" is emphatic in the Greek; it refers to the statement in verse 17.

The Greek word translated "commonwealth" (v. 20) means the constitution or manner of life of a city or state. In ancient times, all people drew from the spirit and laws of the commonwealth to which they belonged. Each individual was conscious of being a member of his or her city or state. The city or state's laws determined the citizen's duties and rights. When a citizen went to another city or country, that person felt himself/herself to be a stranger, and others viewed the individual as such. Paul used this concept to indicate that true Christians were citizens of heaven. Through Christ, the believers' city had been opened to them; they were living in two realms at the same time. Locally, they were citizens of the world; spiritually, they were citizens of heaven. These two realms were not opposed to one another necessarily. (See Rom. 13:1-7.) They became so when the earthly realm attempted to usurp the place which belonged to the heavenly realm.

Paul chose an appropriate figure to express the truth of the Christian's dual citizenship. Philippi was a Roman colony. A Roman colony was the city of Rome transplanted into some part of the Empire. The colonists went out with the pride of Roman citizens to represent and reproduce the city of Rome in the midst of an alien population. Roman colonies often were visited by the emperor. The people in the colonies always were prepared for an unannounced visit by the emperor. One of the titles used for the Roman emperor was savior. Paul told the Philippian Christians that they should await the coming of "a Savior, the Lord Jesus Christ" (v. 20).

In verse 21, Paul described what will happen to the Christian at Christ's coming. The risen Christ lives now in his resplendent body. When he comes, he will change the living saints' bodies to match his glorious body. The word "body" in verse 21 means the self. It is one of nine words used in the New Testament to refer to the whole person. The whole person will be refashioned from what he or she now is into the likeness of what the Savior is. In humiliation, Christ shared our likeness on earth; in exaltation, he awaits our sharing his likeness in glory. The guarantee of this is his "power" that "enables him even to subject all things to himself" (v. 21).

Paul already had stated that the Christians gradually were being conformed during life to the death of Christ (v. 10). In verse 21, he stated that this conformity ultimately will be completed. The change which Christians will undergo will not be merely an external one but will affect their whole form and mode of existence. Christians will become like the body of Christ's glory. This is the expectation of those whose commonwealth is in heaven and who look forward with readiness and longing to the coming of their Savior.

Paul did not think of Christians' eternal blessedness in terms of a separation of a soul from a body. Salvation is not the survival of a soul in the Greek sense but the fullness of life of the whole person. Paul did not teach that the body of flesh would survive or be restored to enter into eternal life. On the contrary, he taught that "flesh and blood cannot inherit the kingdom of God, nor does the perishable inherit the imperishable.... For this perishable nature must put on the imperishable, and this mortal nature must put on immortality" (1 Cor. 15:50,53).

Standing Firm in the Lord
Philippians 4:1 logically belongs to chapter 3; to regard it as drawing the conclusion from 3:17-21 seems best. In effect, Paul gave three motives for his readers to stand firm: (1) his example; (2) their heavenly citizenship and glorious hope; and (3) the all-sufficiency of God's power. They were to be true to their Christian ideals and profession. This was a sincere and moving compliment and appeal.

The Philippian Christians were to "stand firm" in the Lord (4:1). The Greek word translated "stand firm" was used to describe a soldier standing firm in the midst of battle, with the enemy surging down on him. The believers were in the midst of the "enemies of the cross of Christ" (3:18). The Christians were in real danger; they were experiencing pressure. Consequently, they needed to "stand firm" and to pursue the citizenship life which pleased God.

Paul declared that he loved and longed for the Philippian "brethren." They were in his heart and mind. He called them his "joy and crown." Even at that time, they were a source of true gladness; and they were the badge and proof of his service. They were the witnesses to his triumphant ministry.

Paul always was ready to acknowledge the good in those to whom he wrote, even if he found much in them to reprove. However, to no other Christians did he pay such glowing tribute as to those in Philippi. Almost without exception, they were a joy to him. He thought of them, prayed for them, and wrote to them. They were his "crown" of victory.

No Christian Has Freedom to Destroy Fellowship
(4:2-3)

Some disagreement had arisen between two members of the church in Philippi, and Paul urged them to resolve their differences in a manner becoming true Christians (v. 2). Whatever the nature of the disagreement, it was well known in the church because Paul did not hesitate to deal with it publicly. His desire to avoid the slightest appearance of favoritism probably caused him to repeat the verb "entreat." He addressed the two women in

exactly the same terms. Paul did not exhort one to be reconciled to the other, but he appealed to each to work at reconciliation. His exhortation took the form of a direct, personal appeal to those who were chiefly at fault. Perhaps in the difficulty between the two women we may discover the reason for Paul's frequent and earnest exhortations to unity.

The name "Euodia" (literally, prosperous journey) means sweet savor or fragrance. The name "Syntyche" means good luck, fortunate. Both of these women evidently were persons of high standing in the church, possibly deaconesses (see Rom. 16:1), who had been of great service in establishing the church. The cause of their dissension is unknown. The cause may have been a difference in the interpretation of the doctrine of Christian perfection. It may have been the women's energy and activity which occasioned some friction. They had not managed the disagreement wisely. They had allowed the disagreement to deepen into dislike and distrust, and the estrangement had affected the fellowship of the church.

The exhortation "to agree in the Lord" indicates that the desired agreement should be sought on the highest ground and from the loftiest motives. The two women should remember their common relationship to Christ and to his church. As members of the body of Christ, they should put aside jealousy and ill will; they should resolve to understand each other and to seek peace. Their disagreement was not "in the Lord." Christ has one mind; they should seek to possess that mind.

Paul added to his appeal to Euodia and Syntyche a request that "true yokefellow" aid the two women in their efforts at reconciliation (v. 3). This public appeal to a third party showed how strongly Paul desired the reconciliation.

Many guesses have been made as to the identity of "yokefellow." Among the guesses are Luke, Lydia, Silas, Epaphroditus, Timothy, the pastor in Philippi, Sunzugos (a transliteration of the Greek term for yokefellow, taken as a proper name), Paul's wife, and the husband of Euodia or Syntyche. The yokefellow was someone who was well known as Paul's co-worker. He also was in such a conspicuous position that the readers would know who Paul meant. He probably was a prominent member of the church, a man of influence who was esteemed by the people. Like Paul, he must have been a man of extraordinary tact.

In order to emphasize his request, Paul characterized Euodia and Syntyche as persons who had been of great service to him. The word "labored" is a translation of a Greek word used to describe an athletic team who played together, cooperating with one another in harmony to win a victory. The word also has the idea of agonizing and strenuous effort.

"Clement" doubtless was someone who was well known among the Philippian Christians. Paul associated the two women with Clement as having been real helpers in the gospel so that their claim to attention would be appreciated better.

Paul mentioned three of his fellow workers, and he wished to associate them with others whom he did not want to name. Lest any of these should be offended by the omission of their names, he reminded them that their names were inscribed in a better place—in the book of life.

The "book of life" is an Old Testament symbol for God's recognition of those who belong to him (Ex. 32:32; Ps. 69:28; Isa. 4:3; Ezek. 13:9; Dan. 12:1). The figure originally was drawn from the registers of the tribes of Israel. In the New Testament, the expression seems to embody the figurative conception of a register of all who share eternal life through faith in Jesus Christ. (See Luke 10:20; Rev. 3:5; 13:8; 17:8.)

God knows his own for time and eternity. They are "enrolled in heaven" (Heb. 12:23). Possibly, as used in 4:4 by Paul, the expression indicated that these "fellow workers" no longer were alive. However, living or dead, they formed a memorable company of faithful laborers who had been associated with Paul in establishing and keeping peace in the Philippian church.

Lessons for Life from the Scriptures

Christians live in a creative tension. We are aware that we are imperfect, weak, and sinful. Yet, we are conscious of the goal toward which we move: the demand of Christ who said, "You, therefore, must be perfect, as your heavenly Father is perfect" (Matt. 5:48). Maturity is a recognition of this tension and movement toward the goal we see in the perfect One. We live in awareness of a "not yet" that motivates us to renewed effort to cooperate with the One who works in us.

The strongest motivation for high moral standards is Christ's presence in a life. An awareness of his redeeming love and sustaining grace gives incentive for us to show by our conduct that we are friends of the cross. Christ makes us aware that the freedom he gives is freedom to respond to him in all of life's circumstances. He gives no liberty from restraint, discipline, or high principles. He grants us freedom to become all that he can make us.

To disrupt the fellowship of Christ's people is a serious matter. In any church, differences of opinion will arise, but to let these grow into bitterness and hostility is to contribute to a fragmenting of fellowship. Love does not insist on its own way; it negotiates in kindness in a real attempt to determine and do God's will. We are called on to exercise our gifts, not to get our way or to wield power in order to win in our game-playing.

Personal Learning Activities

1. Paul seems to have addressed three problems in the Philippian church. From the following list, select the correct responses.

   _____ (1) Perfectionism
   _____ (2) Poor theology
   _____ (3) Distortions in worship
   _____ (4) Antinomianism
   _____ (5) Lack of leadership
   _____ (6) Disunity

2. In refuting the concept of a sinless level of Christian life, Paul used the metaphor of a _____ .

3. The prize toward which Paul moved was (choose one):

   _____ (1) The recognition of his peers
   _____ (2) The upward call of God in Christ Jesus
   _____ (3) Heaven
   _____ (4) Commendation from God

4. To Paul, the enemies of the cross were (choose the correct answer):

   _____ (1) The Jews
   _____ (2) The pagans
   _____ (3) The Judaizers
   _____ (4) Christians who viewed liberty as license

5. Match the following two lists by pairing the terms with their correct definitions.

   _____ (1) Heaven
   _____ (2) Euodia
   _____ (3) Syntyche
   _____ (4) Yokefellow
   _____ (5) Clement
   _____ (6) Book of life
   _____ (7) Commonwealth
   _____ (8) Body

   (a) Good fortune
   (b) Had labored side by side with Paul
   (c) The whole self
   (d) Roll of those who share in eternal life
   (e) Sweet fragrance
   (f) Called on to be a peacemaker
   (g) Realm of which Christians are citizens
   (h) Citizenship, manner of life

123

9

Final Admonitions, Greetings, and Gratitude

Philippians 4:4-23

In the conclusion of the Philippian letter, Paul dealt with a variety of subjects. In 4:4-7, he renewed his exhortation to rejoice. The joy which he had in mind was not something that could be realized in life's external conditions or in some state of mind. On the contrary, it could be seized as a reality by faith alone. "Joy" as Paul meant it was "in" (Rom. 14:17) or "by" (1 Thess. 1:6) the Holy Spirit. It was conferred on believers as Christ's joy.

Joy, although a gift from Christ, never is realized fully; it always lies ahead of the Christian as something to be realized. Joy never can become a static condition. It becomes real in the act of faith, and it enables believers to overcome the sorrow that assails them in the world (John 16:20-22).

Jesus Christ was "a man of sorrows, and acquainted with grief" (Isa. 53:3); yet, he possessed a deep joy that was beyond anything the world could offer. The writer of Hebrews indicated that Jesus "for the joy that was set before him endured the cross, despising the shame" (Heb. 12:2).

The Christian's existence is an existence in joy. It is a fruit of the Spirit second only to love (Gal. 5:22). It is a quality of the Christian life which gives a new glow to life.

In 4:8-9, Paul urged his readers to fill their thoughts with things that were good and holy and to translate into action the lessons they had learned from him. He gave them a rule to guide their thoughts; he already had exhibited in his life a rule to guide their conduct.

People are thinking beings. We all have ideas; we see the world about us and remember what we see. From the facts which we experience, we make inferences, draw conclusions, and make these the bases of our actions. We have the power of governing our thoughts, so we are responsible for them. If thoughts are ordered well, outward conduct will follow.

In 4:10-20, Paul expressed his gratitude for the gift he had received from the Philippian Christians. They had heard of his condition in prison. Their sympathy was awakened, and they promptly sent an offering to him.

Paul was not destitute, but he had to meet the expenses of his maintenance in Rome, which included renting a house. (See Acts 28:30.) When his plight became known to the Philippian Christians, they responded immediately.

Previously, when Paul had been in need the Philippian church had helped him. When those needs had been met, their offerings had ceased. Their love for him had not decreased; they simply did not know of his need. When they learned of his situation in Rome, they sent help. They also wrote a letter of sympathy. They deplored their apparent neglect and assured him that it had not been caused by a lack of love and appreciation but entirely by their ignorance of his needs. They sent the letter and the gift by Epaphroditus.

In 4:21-23, Paul saluted "every saint," sent greetings from the brethren at Rome, and closed with a benediction.

Renewed Exhortations to Joy (4:4-7)

Joy in the Lord

In verse 4, the keynote of the epistle is sounded again. The verb form in Greek is an imperative. Originally, this command to rejoice may have been related to the dissension between Euodia and Syntyche, for nothing can destroy gladness of heart as surely as contention and misunderstanding. More likely, however, in this last series of admonitions, Paul may have given his dear friends an informal summary of the whole spirit and conduct of the Christian life. Today, Christians' rejoicing in the Lord is a direct result of their faith. If the Lord is what believers hold him to be, then Christ offers more to make them glad than anyone or anything else can do to make them sorry.

Paul indicated that the Philippian Christians were to rejoice always, not simply at certain periods. The word "always" is emphatic in the Greek, and the command is strengthened by repetition. Paul stressed that they were to rejoice under all circumstances. No matter what sacrifices they had to make, what trials they had to bear, or what losses they had to sustain, they were to rejoice. Today, to rejoice always, no matter what the circumstances of life are, is difficult. However, Christian joy is independent of circumstances because its source is in Christ's presence.

Paul's command was to "rejoice in the Lord" (v. 4), for he realized that Christians live in a sphere that is not recognizable by their five senses. However, it is ever present to faith. Therefore, "in Christ" alone lies the source of true and lasting joy. This kind of joy requires deep faith and close union with Christ. This joy is possible only to those who are conscious that they live in the unseen and eternal.

Paul had learned how to "rejoice in the Lord always" (v. 4). He was "sorrowful, yet always rejoicing" (2 Cor. 6:10). He was aware that Christ's Spirit was in him, so he could not be downcast, even in jail. In Philippi, he and Silas had demonstrated this joy even after they had been beaten publicly and put in the inner prison with their feet fastened in stocks (Acts 16:23-24). At the time Paul wrote the Philippian letter, he was in prison again; he had been in prison for about four years. He was dependent on others for a living, misunderstood and opposed by many fellow-Christians, and uncertain about the outcome of his trial. Yet in all this darkness, he rejoiced "in the Lord." This special kind of joy could not have been merely a temperamental buoyancy of vigorous health, worldly comfort, or success.

The Old Testament contains many commands to Israel to rejoice in the Lord. Usually, the grounds given for rejoicing were God's revealed character—especially his mercy and grace—and the fact that he was Israel's God. The prophet Habakkuk (3:17-18) said that in spite of the terror produced by hostile invasion, the true Israelite was blessed with the hope of salvation and joy in the Lord.

Jesus experienced sorrow, yet he rejoiced. Joy sprang from his great, loving heart like water from an artesian well; he yearned to share his joy with the sad hearts around him. (See John 17:13.) Even in the upper room, with the cross only a few hours away, he said to his disciples: "These things I have spoken to you, that my joy may be in you, and that your joy may be full" (John 15:11).

Christian Tolerance
Paul urged the Philippians, "Let all men know your forbearance" (v. 5). The Greek word translated "forbearance" (epieikes) is difficult to translate into English. This difficulty can be seen in the number of English words used to translate it. It has been translated yieldingness, moderation, considerateness, magnanimity, softness, and gentleness. The Greek word was used to express the disposition which contented itself with less than its due and shrank from insisting on its strict rights. It expressed a mind-set opposed to the eager overrating of personal worth or objects and opposed to the arrogance that insists on its will. The word describes the attitude which forgets self in favor of others and willingly yields purely personal claims. It denotes the spirit that enables Christians to bear injuries with patience and to resist demanding all that is rightly their due. (See 1 Cor. 6:7.) The word conveys the quality which leads believers to yield rather than insist on the full measure of their rights, to suffer wrong rather than to do wrong.

The believers' "forbearance" was to be known to "all men" (v. 5). This essential Christian spirit was to be so conspicuous a feature of their character that it would be known to all people with whom they came in contact. To enforce the command, Paul added the words, "The Lord is at hand." The words "at hand" translate a Greek word which literally means near. The word may refer to the second coming and its near approach; it also may be an expression of Paul's agreement with the psalmist: "The Lord is near to all who call upon him" (Ps. 145:18). If the latter is what Paul had in mind, he meant that the Lord is near in the sense of his abiding presence with Christians.

The Threat of Overanxiety
In verse 6, Paul admonished the Philippian Christians to turn, with the confidence of little children, to their loving heavenly Father who gives "good things to those who ask him" (Matt. 7:11). He commanded them to "have no anxiety about anything." He did not mean that they were to exercise no care about worldly matters. They were to exercise confidence in God who would free them from anxiety. The root idea of the Greek word translated "anxiety" is a divided mind. It describes the mind as

looking two ways and not being able to find a place where it can settle down. The Greek construction indicates a prohibition of the continuance of an action going on habitually. The Philippian Christians already were anxious.

Paul's command repeated Jesus' command to his disciples, "Do not be anxious" (Matt. 6:25). He directed his prohibition to all who, in mere self-dependence, felt alone and painfully anxious amid life's difficulties and dangers. To care was a virtue; but to be overanxious, destructive. This painful anxiety was not trust in God; it was self-trust which produced inward suffering, fear, and worry.

From a human point of view, Paul had plenty to be anxious about. He was not certain whether he would be set free or be sentenced to die. The Philippian Christians had ample cause for anxiety regarding their circumstances. Paul did not write about imaginary troubles or unreal anxieties; he dealt with serious threats and difficulties. His command to his readers was not designed to make light of their troubles but to affirm that God was greater than all their troubles.

Overanxiety is an emotional illness, and an illness needs a cure. Paul prescribed a treatment: prayer and commitment of life to God. The Greek word translated "prayer" is a general word conveying the ideas of adoration, devotion, and worship. It does not refer to petitions but to the mood of the petitioner. "Prayer" describes a frame of mind or an attitude. When Christians find themselves anxious, their first action ought to be to get alone with God and worship him.

The word "supplication" is a more specific term than "prayer." It is a word used to designate a single feature of prayer: petition for necessities. The term describes sharing of needs and problems with God. God does not need to be informed of our necessities, but we need to express them to him. Thanksgiving is a necessary part of prayer, and it never should be absent from worship. Some anxieties can resist everything except thanksgiving. Karl Barth wrote: "Thanksgiving means giving God the glory in everything, making room for him, casting our care on him, letting it be his care. The troubles that exercise us then cease to be hidden and bottled up. They are so to speak laid open towards God, spread out before him."[1]

God's Peace
A blessing awaits Christians who take all their anxieties to God

in prayer. The "peace of God" will keep their "hearts and minds in Christ Jesus" (v. 7). The peace of God, first of all, is the peace which God possesses. (See Rom. 15:33; 1 Cor. 14:33; Phil. 4:9.) Then it is the peace which he bestows on all who do what Paul had urged in the preceding verses. God is not beset with anxieties, for he never is at the mercy of circumstances. If Christians are content to trust God and leave all the circumstances of life to him, God imparts his peace.

The "peace of God" is boundless and cannot be captured in our verbal nets. Therefore, when we seek to express our understanding of what God's peace is and implies, we always fall short. God's peace is so great, so high, so overpowering, so divine, that it passes all understanding. No one can explain peace; it must be experienced to be known. Its calm blessedness transcends the reach of human thought. God's peace can be received but not understood. Moreover, God's peace is independent of external conditions. No one or nothing can give it except God. (See Isa. 26:3.)

The Greek word translated "will keep" (v. 7) is a military term for sentry duty. As a garrison of soldiers, God's peace will possess the responsive believer's heart and mind. Like a sentinel on duty, God's peace will stand guard before the door of the inner self to keep back all intruders who would break in on the integrity of a believer's thoughts.

The heart and mind can be preserved in peace only "in Christ Jesus" (v. 7). Paul never lost sight of the truth that all a believer's security and blessedness were to be traced to Christ. What he meant was that in Christ, who is the one true, spiritual region or sphere of blessing, God's peace will protect the heart and mind against all foes.

Exhortation to Practice What Is Noblest and Best (4:8-9)

In 4:4-7, Paul wrote of God's peace which, like a sentry, keeps the Christian's heart with its affections and thoughts. In 4:8-9, he wrote of the God of peace. The two emphases in these verses are thinking and doing.

As a Christian Thinks

In verse 8, Paul repeated the "finally" of 3:1. He seemed to have prepared repeatedly to conclude his letter, but for him to say farewell to his beloved friends was not easy. In verse 8, he appealed to them to give their minds suitable material to work on.

The Christian's thoughts are important because they have a reflex effect on character. If the believer ignores the indwelling Christ and cherishes evil thoughts, that person deteriorates in character. Paul stated this principle clearly when he wrote that because the Gentiles refused to honor God, "they became futile in their thinking and their senseless minds were darkened" (Rom. 1:21). When believers perpetually cherish unholy, impure, and untrue thoughts, they will become unholy, impure, and untrue Christians. Character takes on the complexion and hue of thinking.

Christians who cherish noble thoughts become more noble. If they are generous in their thoughts, they will be generous in acts. Believers who are loving and tender in their thoughts will be loving and tender in their bearing. If Christians allow the indwelling Christ to take care of their thoughts, their thoughts will mold character reflectively and unconsciously into more Christlike persons.

Paul called some of the suitable materials for the Christian's mind to work on excellent and "worthy of praise" (v. 8). These terms include what is noble towards God, what is purifying to the believer, and what commends itself to the highest aspirations of other Christians. The first virtue which Paul mentioned was "whatever is true." The word "true" includes both speech and fact; it refers to everything that is the reverse of falsehood. The term denotes not only veracity and fidelity, but also whatever in conduct and mental disposition God's truth requires as agreeable to itself. Paul exhorted his readers to think about truth, especially the highest of all truths, the truth concerning God and their relation to him.

The second virtue which Paul mentioned in his catalog was "whatever is honorable." The Greek word translated "honorable" (semna) is found in the New Testament only in verse 8 and four times in the pastoral epistles. It is a difficult word to translate into English. The term sometimes is translated respectable, reverent, venerable, or honest. The word points to a Christian decorum, a self-respect, which is consistent with true humility.

The third concept which Paul gave for the Philippian Christians to think about was "whatever is just" (v. 8). The word "just" refers to righteousness in its widest meaning. It means being right and doing right. It refers to the duty or obligation that rightfully is due to God and to people.

The fourth virtue for the Philippian Christians to consider was "whatever is pure" (v. 8). The word "pure" described a person who recoiled from the faintest shade or slightest infection of iniquity. It was used in the special sense of chastity of thought and act involving the body.

The fifth idea Paul gave his readers to think about was "whatever is lovely" (v. 8). The word "lovely" described that which was pleasing or acceptable. It delineated that which drew out love, cherished love, and befitted love.

The last conception which Paul gave for the Philippian Christians to think about was "whatever is gracious" (v. 8). The word "gracious" sometimes is translated good report. It could refer to things of which people spoke well. In addition, the term had an active sense—speaking in such a way as to emphasize that which was favorable about anything.

Of the six virtues, the first two describe the subjects of thought in themselves; the second pair relates to practical life; and the last pair relates to the results which right thinking produces in Christians.

The mind drilled to dwell on things which have divine approval is the surest way of increasing the newness of life. Christians cannot afford to waste mind power on thoughts that tear them down or that would tear others down if those thoughts were shared with them. The profitable objects for Christians' mental concentration are those which are true, honorable, just, pure, lovely, and gracious.

A Human Model

The exemplary life, including all the qualities which Paul had enumerated in verse 8, was expressed fully in Christ. However, if Christ's life seemed too remote, Paul dared to direct his Philippian friends to a measurable realization of his (Paul's) character (v. 9).

Paul suggested two avenues for guiding his readers' behavior. First, he introduced the instruction that he gave them during his ministry among them. Paul was careful about his educational ministry to the newborn Christians. When the Philippians were converted, he was concerned about their spiritual growth. So, he developed a teaching program. They "learned" the gospel as a matter of information and they "received" it as a matter of personal experience (v. 9). Paul urged them to follow the instructions which they had received.

Second, Paul commended to the Philippian Christians the concrete example which he had demonstrated for their pattern of Christian living. Paul had taught them by word and by his living. When Paul was present, they saw a pattern of Christian life; when he was absent, they heard concerning that pattern of life. Jesus had set them an example; however, to follow in his footsteps was not easy. In Paul's ministry among them, he had taught and lived the gospel so that the Philippian Christians could see the truth in his life. He tried to follow Christ's steps. So he told his readers that if they were following him, they would be following Christ.

For the Philippian Christians to know the truth was not enough; they should do the truth. They must translate into action the lessons which they had learned from Paul's teaching and example.

Paul promised the Philippian Christians that as a result of a life of pure thoughts and right actions, the God of peace would be with them. God dwells with those who think holy thoughts and do right deeds, and he brings his peace.

Paul's Gratitude for the Gift (4:10-20)

A Reviving of Care
Paul had not thanked the Philippian Christians pointedly for their gift which was, in all likelihood, the Philippian letter's immediate occasion. The fact that he accepted their gift showed his confidence in their love. To receive support from his converts was his right as a minister of the gospel, but he seldom laid claim to his right.

The Philippian Christians sent the gift for which Paul felt so much gratitude. However, he regarded "the Lord" as its source and rejoiced in it as an expression of the Lord's kindness (v. 10). In his mind, the experience was associated with joy. He was convinced that the Lord had given the Philippian Christians the idea—to send the gift to him.

At least among some of the Philippian Christians, concern for Paul was ever present. Apparently, however, for them to communicate with him or to send help as they desired was not always easy. Yet, when the opportunity did not permit them to give assistance, the will to help always was present.

Paul knew that his Philippian friends were concerned about him during his stay in the Caesarean and Roman prisons. But circumstances had not given them opportunity to express their concern. They had sent him gifts; but for some reason beyond their control, a long interval had preceded the last gift.

In expressing his appreciation, Paul used the image of a tree or a plant which had been barren in the winter. Then it sprouted new shoots or flowers in the spring. For a long time, the Philippian Christians were barren in expressing their care for him; now they were blossoming anew with thoughts for his welfare. He declared that their barrenness was not due to a lack of concern but of opportunity.

The Lesson of Contentment

Paul quickly indicated that he was not complaining (v. 11). He assured his friends that his peace and joy did not depend on circumstances or things. His peace and joy came from something deeper, something apart from poverty or prosperity. He had learned under all circumstances to be content with what he had, inwardly to be independent of outward circumstances. He did not indicate that he had learned the lesson all at once. Probably the experiences of four years of imprisonment had taught him patience. The "I" is emphatic (v. 11), stressing his position and implying an appeal to his readers to learn the secret.

Paul did not pretend that he liked being in want, and he did not imply that hunger and privation were better than plenty. What he indicated was that in any circumstance, through Christ's power, he could do the work for which Christ had called him. He did not depend on any state of affairs or on other people for strength to deal with any situation. Doubtless, he often was in circumstances of necessity, but he had learned to cope with them so that they did not give him great uneasiness.

Paul had learned to be calm and confident in the midst of the most disturbing circumstances. Particularly, he had refused to allow his joy and peace to be dependent on material possessions and physical comforts.

Paul's sufficiency was not the Stoic kind; it was not self-sufficiency. He found his sufficiency in Christ. He was independent of circumstances because he was dependent on Christ. His sense of need aroused his desire for spiritual growth. To be content with his spiritual state would not have allowed him to make spiritual progress. God did not expect Paul to be content with unsatisfactory conditions when God had better ones for him. However, in all circumstances God was ready to supply Paul with contentment of mind.

In verse 12, Paul added several amplifying clauses to emphasize the self-sufficiency that he had expressed in verse 11. He explained that he had arrived at this secret of contentment as one initiated into a secret order. Through trial and testing, he had been initiated into the wonderful secret of contentment in spite of prosperity or poverty.

Paul knew theoretically the difficulty of living a godly life with plenty, and he knew it experientially. Probably he was wealthy when he was converted. Though he had known plenty, he had overcome the difficulty presented by plenty. He also had experienced privation and want, and he had learned to live with them without discontent. He had been initiated into the experience of both abundance and need, and he had learned how to bear either safely. He had been able to do this in the power by which he lived his whole life: strength given by union with Christ. His contentment did not come by nature, but by grace.

In verse 13, Paul traced his ability to be independent of circumstances to its true source: the indwelling Christ. He did not think of himself as a strong man who needed no support. He had schooled himself to be independent of outward circumstances, but he was aware of his dependence on Christ and the strength which Christ supplied. Paul was weak, but he had Christ's presence; in the strength of that presence, he could do all things. (See 2 Cor. 12:9-10).

The power of the living Christ within enabled Paul to exhibit the spirit of contentment and to "do all things" that he should do as Christ's minister (v. 13). The words point to a real supply of strength, not to a mere sense of courage. He was not granted power to gratify his desires or to accomplish selfish plans. He was granted the power for whatever Christ wished him to do. This internal work of the Spirit is not to be understood as a complete transformation of personality or as the displacement of something human by something divine. It is to be understood as an inflow of divine power accomplishing a reorientation of a person's will toward God.

Paul verbally identified the risen Lord with the Spirit: "The Lord is the Spirit" (2 Cor. 3:17). The Holy Spirit was the manner in which the living Christ worked in Paul's life and ministry. Not only did the Holy Spirit create his faith, enabling him to accept

Christ as his Lord and Savior, but he dwelt within Paul, enabling him to live according to the Spirit. Drawing on the inner resources which were his in Christ, Paul found meaning and fulfillment as his outward circumstances changed from day to day. This was the testimony of a man in Christ, a man who felt himself possessed by a power stronger than himself. This power sustained his faith, hope, and sense of purpose in all circumstances.

The Ministry of Support

By the word "yet" (v. 14), Paul indicated that in declaring his independence of human assistance he was not disparaging his Philippian friends' gift. He did not wish to give the impression that their gift was not necessary or welcomed. He had written that he was content under all circumstances, but he was careful not to leave the notion that the gift had been superfluous and that he did not appreciate it. On the contrary, he stated that he definitely was pleased with it.

In sending the gift, the Philippian Christians had shared in Paul's affliction (v. 14). They had made his distress theirs. They had sympathized with him in his affliction and had assisted him in bearing it. The word "share" is a form of the word for fellowship. The church entered into a fellowship of giving and receiving. The church gave materially to Paul and received spiritually from the Lord. In this sharing, Paul's friends received the greater blessing. He received the lesser blessing and rejoiced that it was so.

The gift that Epaphroditus brought to Paul in Rome was not the first or the only assistance the Philippian Christians gave him (v. 15). At the time of their first acquaintance with the gospel, they showed the same spirit of giving which was in contrast to the other churches that Paul founded. When the gospel was preached for the first time in Macedonia and Greece, the Philippian Christians supported him as he preached in other cities. (See 2 Cor. 11:9.) Only the Philippian church had been allowed the privilege of entering into a partnership of "giving and receiving" (v. 15). Paul did not imply blame of other churches. The thought is that of a sure and early proof of the Philippian Christians' participation with him in his ministry.

As a general policy, Paul did not accept financial help to meet his needs and the needs of impoverished Christian communities where he labored. He did not earn his living by preaching the gospel. He devoted the major part of his time to his ministry, but he also had a secular trade: tentmaking. He expressed pride that by the skill of his hands, he could earn his way without having to depend on the churches' gifts. In Thessalonica, he accepted no support from the Thessalonians. At Corinth, he accepted no gifts from the Corinthians (2 Cor. 11:7; 12:13). For some reason, however, Paul did not refuse to accept financial help from the Philippian church. This fact suggests a relationship of mutual trust, an intimate bond.

The Greek words translated "giving and receiving" (v. 15) are technical terms derived from the language of bookkeeping. This was Paul's imaginative way of expressing his sense of obligation. This was his only church in which mutual services had been rendered. Paul received material gifts through them and they received spiritual gifts through him.

Before and after Paul left Macedonia and while he was still in Thessalonica, the Philippian Christians sent "help once and again" (v. 16). Thessalonica was the capital of Macedonia located about 100 miles from Philippi on the Egnatian Way. It was a city of far greater importance and wealth than Philippi. When the Philippian Christians heard of Paul's troubles in Thessalonica (Acts 17:1-9), they immediately rushed to his aid, enabling him to continue his work there.

The Blessing of Giving
Paul's fear of being misunderstood when he wrote about receiving money appears again and again, no doubt, because his enemies constantly were misrepresenting his motives. If he accepted a gift, or if his enemies suspected that he had, they probably accused him of preaching for money. If he did not accept pay, they likely accused him of making a show of humility.

Paul's reference to the Philippian Christians' past liberality might cause them to conclude that he coveted their gifts. He corrected this possible misunderstanding at once. He appreciated the gift, not only for his sake but even more because of what it meant to his Philippian friends. He was convinced that money given for Christ's work blessed the one who gave it more than the one who received it. (See Acts 20:35.) The image of "fruit" (v. 17) to denote results was used because Christians reap or gather the fruit of that which they plant. Paul desired the fruit of spiritual enrichment among the Philippian Christians.

Just what was included in the gift never was indicated. It probably included money, clothes, books, and so on. Whatever was included, Paul interpreted it as "a fragrant offering, a sacrifice acceptable and pleasing to God" (v. 18). It was comparable to the whole burnt offering which the Israelites brought to God. (See Lev. 1:9.) The Philippian Christians had made the offering, not merely from personal friendship, but because Paul was Christ's minister. Paul felt that it would be acceptable to Christ.

In the first part of verse 18, Paul used commercial language. He wrote that he had received in full; nothing more was due him. He did not want his readers to think that he was asking for more. In the last part of verse 18, he adopted the language of sacrifice. The gift was an offering laid on the altar of God, brought to God.

Paul assured the Philippian Christians that as they had supplied his needs as God's servant, God would supply their needs "according to his riches in glory in Christ Jesus" (v. 19). They had supplied his needs, and he only could thank them; but God would supply all their needs. In Christ, full provision is available for all the needs of God's people. Paul simply was repeating what he wrote at greater length to the Corinthian Christians when he noted the Philippian Christians' generosity toward the poor saints in Jerusalem (2 Cor. 9:1-15). He told the Corinthian believers that no gift to the work of God ever made a person poorer.

Though Paul actually never had expressed thanks, he had given moving testimony of his profound appreciation for the gift and of the loving spirit which prompted it. The thought of God in verse 19 led him to break into a doxology with which 4:10-20 fittingly concludes (v. 20). Paul wrote: May our God and Father receive glory. "Glory" is manifested excellence. The glory which Paul ascribed to God is praise to God when he is known for who he is. Moreover, this glory is to be "for ever and ever" (v. 20). In this phrase, Paul expressed the idea of eternity. The word "amen" expressed approval of what had been written and was an expression of confirmation and assurance.

Farewell Words (4:21-23)

For Paul to close his epistles with affectionate salutations to various members of the churches to which he was writing was customary. These salutations usually were specific and mentioned the names of church members. In Philippians, the salutation is general; no members are specified by name.

Paul expressed his loving concern for each member in the church, not simply the company of believers as a whole (v. 21). He even included those who were censured in 2:20-21. All the members had one thing in common, and yet they were so amazingly different in so many ways. Some had made little progress in Christian growth since conversion. Others professed a lofty spirituality but lacked the spirit of loving unity. Some had come to a high level of spiritual experience and were able to appreciate the deepest teachings of the nature of Christ. Some had been generous and thoughtful. However, that they were "in Christ Jesus" so that Paul could include them all in his salutation as "saints" was enough.

In verse 22, Paul referred to the wider circle of believers in Rome and described them as "saints" among whom "those of Caesar's household" received special mention. The phrase "Caesar's household" referred to the whole multitude of persons in the emperor's service, whether enslaved or free. That Paul had added from this group new converts to the church is possible. He may have mentioned this fact in order to show the Philippian Christians that his imprisonment had given opportunity for the spread of the gospel.

Paul concluded his letter with a benediction or pronouncement of grace (v. 23). What Paul especially desired for his favorite church was that they might possess "the grace." The letter begins with grace (1:2) and ends with grace. It is the grace "of the Lord Jesus Christ" (4:20). The singular "spirit" reflects the thought that they all were animated by one spirit. The best way to conclude the study of Paul's letter to his dear friends in Philippi is to reflect on his statement: "The grace of the Lord Jesus Christ be with your spirit."

Lessons for Life from the Scriptures

Overanxiety fragments life and is a denial of Christ's ability to help us deal with life's dynamics. To worry is not a sin. Worry can be constructive if concern moves us to positive action. To become overanxious about temporal matters to the point that we come apart at the seams is destructive and is the opposite of faith. Faith does the best it knows to do in any circumstance, asking that God work with and beyond human strength. Peace comes when we realize that God shares our good and bad moments in active care.

We are—or we become—what we think about. Thoughts are the springs of attitudes and acts. That on which we concentrate will claim our energies to attain, to get. The materials of our thinking must be of superlative quality if we are to be quality persons. Christ could have sat for the portrait Paul painted of excellence in thinking. Christ possessed all the virtues listed by Paul. How much thought do we give to Christ's revelation concerning God and true humanity?

Sharing in the spirit of Christ issues in mutual blessing. The grace of receiving allows another to experience the joy of giving. The grace of giving increases the capacity of generosity and meets real needs of those receiving. To give or to receive is not always easy, but supportive ministry is imperative to Christian growth.

---

1. Karl Barth, *The Epistle to the Philippians* (Richmond: John Knox Press, 1962), pp. 122-23.

Personal Learning Activities

1. To Paul, joy was (choose one):
   _____ (1) Found in external conditions, circumstances
   _____ (2) A static condition
   _____ (3) A quality of the Christian life effected through faith
   _____ (4) The absence of sorrow
2. Match the following two lists by pairing the terms with their proper definitions.
   _____ (1) Anxiety   (a) God's gift to believers
   _____ (2) Forbearance (b) Sphere of blessing
   _____ (3) Supplication (c) A divided mind
   _____ (4) Peace   (d) Sentry duty, stand guard
   _____ (5) Keep   (e) Petition for specific needs
   _____ (6) In Christ Jesus (f) Considerateness, magnanimity
3. Paul saw a vital relationship between thinking and character. True _____ False _____

4. Paul encouraged his readers to think about those things that are _____ , _____ , _____ , _____ , _____ , and _____ . (Select the correct answers from the following list.)
   (1) Pure   (5) Pleasant
   (2) Lovely   (6) Just
   (3) True   (7) Honorable
   (4) Profitable (8) Gracious
5. Paul was upset because of the long interval between the Philippian Christians' gifts to him. True _____ False _____

Answers:
1. (3); 2. (1) c, (2) f, (3) e, (4) a, (5) d, (6) b; 3. True; 4. (1), (2), (3), (6), (7), (8); 5. False.

THE CHURCH STUDY COURSE

The Church Study Course consists of a variety of short-term credit courses for adults and youth and noncredit foundational units for children and preschoolers. The materials are for use in addition to the study and training curriculums made available to the churches on an ongoing basis.

Study courses and foundational units are organized into a system that is promoted by the Sunday School Board, 127 Ninth Avenue, North, Nashville, Tennessee 37234; by the Woman's Missionary Union, 600 North Twentieth Street, Birmingham, Alabama 35203; by the Brotherhood Commission, 1548 Poplar Avenue, Memphis, Tennessee 38104; and by the respective departments of the state conventions affiliated with the Southern Baptist Convention.

Study course materials are flexible enough to be adapted to the needs of any Baptist church. The resources are published in several different formats—textbooks of various sizes, workbooks, and kits. Each item contains a brief explanation of the Church Study Course and information on requesting credit. Additional information and interpretation are available from the participating agencies.

Types of Study and Credit

Adults and youth can earn study course credit through individual or group study. Teachers of courses or of foundational units are also eligible to receive credit.

1. Class Experience.—Group involvement with course material for the designated number of hours for the particular course. A person who is absent from one or more sessions must complete the "Personal Learning Activities" or other requirements for the course.
2. Individual Study.—This includes reading, viewing, or listening to course material and completing the specified requirements for the course.
3. Lesson Course Study.—Parallel use of designated study course material during the study of selected units in Church Program Organization periodical curriculum

units. Guidance for this means of credit appears in the selected periodical.

4. Institutional Study.—Parallel use of designated study course material during regular courses at educational institutions, including Seminary Extension Department courses. Guidance for this means of credit is provided by the teacher.

Credit is awarded for the successful completion of a course of study. This credit is granted by the Church Study Course Awards Office, 127 Ninth Avenue, North, Nashville, Tennessee 37234, for the participating agencies. Form 151 (available free) is recommended for use in requesting credit.

When credit is issued to a person on request, the Awards Office sends two copies of a notice of credit earned to the church. The original copy of the credit slip should be filed by the study course clerk in the participant's record of training folder. The duplicate should be given to the person who earned the credit. Accumulated credits are applied toward leadership or member development diplomas, which are measures of learning, growth, development, and training.

Detailed information about the Church Study Course system of credits, diplomas, and record keeping is available from the participating agencies. Study course materials, supplementary teaching or learning aids, and forms for record keeping may be ordered from Baptist Book Stores.

The Church Study Course Curriculum
Credit is granted on those courses listed in the current copy of *Church Services and Materials Catalog* and *Baptist Book Store Catalog*. When selecting courses or foundational units, check the current catalogs to determine what study course materials are valid.

How to Request Credit for This Course
This book is the text for a course in the subject area Bible Study.

This course is designed for 5 hours of group study. Credit is awarded for satisfactory class experience with the study material for the minimum number of hours. A person who is absent from one or more sessions must complete the "Personal Learning Activities" or other requirements for the materials missed.

Credit also is allowed for use of this material in individual study and in institutional study, if so designated.

The following requirements must be met for credit in this course:
1. Read the book *Philippians: Rejoice in the Lord.*
2. Attend at least 5 hours of class study or complete all "Personal Learning Activities" (see end of each chapter). A class member who is absent from one or more class sessions must complete "Personal Learning Activities" on chapters missed. In such a case, he must turn in his paper by the date the teacher sets, usually within ten days following the last class.

Credit in this course may be earned through individual study. The requirements for such credit are:
1. Read the book.
2. Complete the "Personal Learning Activities" on the chapters.

Credit in this course may be earned through study in an educational institution, if so designated by a teacher. The requirements are:
1. Read the book.
2. Fulfill the requirements of the course taught at the institution.

After the course is completed, the teacher, the study course records librarian, the learner, or any person designated by the church should complete Form 151 ("Church Study Course Credit Request, Revised 1975") and send it to the Awards Office, 127 Ninth Avenue, North, Nashville, Tennessee 37234. In the back of this book the reader will find a form which he may cut out, fill in, and send to the Awards Office.

INSTRUCTIONS: If requested by the teacher, fill in this form and give it to him when the course is completed. If preferred, mail this request for course credit to

AWARDS OFFICE
THE SUNDAY SCHOOL BOARD, SBC
127 NINTH AVENUE, NORTH
NASHVILLE, TENNESSEE 37234

State Convention   Association

Indicate Type of Study (X)

☐ Class   ☐ Individual   ☐ Lesson Course   ☐ Educational Institution

CHURCH

Church Name

Mail to (if Different from Church Address)

MAIL TO

Mailing Address

Street, Route, or P.O. Box

City, State, Zip Code

City, State, Zip Code

LAST NAME	FIRST NAME AND MIDDLE INITIAL	MRS. (X)	COURSE TITLE
			Philippians: Rejoice in the Lord